M

Zenith Anthologies

SOULSCRIPT: AFRO-AMERICAN POETRY
Edited by June Jordan

BONDAGE, FREEDOM AND BEYOND:
The Prose of Black Americans
Edited by Addison Gayle, Jr.

TALES & STORIES FOR BLACK FOLKS
Edited by Toni Cade Bambara

The aim of Zenith Books is to present the history and culture of minority groups in the United States and their participation in the growth and development of the country. Through histories, biographies, literature, and the arts, Zenith Books will increase the awareness of and develop an understanding and appreciation for minority group heritage.

Zenith Books Series Consultant: John Hope Franklin
Professor of History, University of Chicago

General Editor: Milton Meltzer

DR. JOHN HOPE FRANKLIN, Professor in the History Department at the University of Chicago, has also taught at Brooklyn College, Fisk University, and Howard University. For the year 1962–63, he was Pitt Professor of American History and Institutions at Cambridge University, in England. He is the author of many books, including *From Slavery to Freedom, The Militant South, Reconstruction After the Civil War,* and *The Emancipation Proclamation.*

MILTON MELTZER is the author of many highly successful books for all age groups. His publications include *In Their Own Words: A History of the American Negro; Langston Hughes, A Biography;* and *Slavery: From the Rise of Western Civilization to the Renaissance.* Mr. Meltzer collaborated with Langston Hughes on *A Pictorial History of the Negro in America* and *Black Magic.*

BLACK SCENES

BLACK SCENES

Edited by Alice Childress *comp.*

ZENITH BOOKS
1971
Doubleday & Company, Inc.
GARDEN CITY, NEW YORK

ACKNOWLEDGMENTS

Thanks are due to the following for permission to include copyrighted selections:

Floyd Barbour for his scene from *The Bird Cage*, Copyright © 1971 by Floyd Barbour.

William Branch for his scene from *To Follow the Phoenix*.

Theodore Browne for his scene from *Natural Man*.

Ed Bullins and The Bobbs-Merrill Company, Inc. for his scene from A SON COME HOME from *Five Plays by Ed Bullins*, Copyright © 1968 by Ed Bullins.

Steve Carter for his scene from *One Last Look*, Copyright © 1970 by Steve Carter.

Alice Childress for her scene from *The African Garden*, Copyright © 1971 by Alice Childress.

Ossie Davis for his scene from *Purlie Victorious*, Copyright © 1961 by Ossie Davis.

Roger Furman for his scene from *To Kill a Devil*.

Random House, Inc. and the William Morris Agency for a scene from *A Raisin in the Sun* by Lorraine Hansberry, Copyright © 1958 by Robert Nemiroff as Executor of the Estate of Lorraine Hansberry as an unpublished work. Copyright © 1959, 1966 by Robert Nemiroff as Executor of the Estate of Lorraine Hansberry.

Prentice-Hall, Inc. and the William Morris Agency for selection from *To Be Young, Gifted and Black: Lorraine Hansberry in Her Own Words* by Robert Nemiroff, Copyright © 1969 by Robert Nemiroff as Executor of the Estate of Lorraine Hansberry.

Abbey Lincoln for her scene from *A Streak o' Lean*, Copyright © 1967 by Abbey Lincoln.

Julian Mayfield for his scene from *"417"*.

Loften Mitchell for his scene from *Land Beyond the River*, Copyright © 1963 by Loften Mitchell.

Ted Shine for his scene from *Shoes*, Copyright © 1971 by Ted Shine.

Curtis Brown, Ltd. for a scene from *Day of Absence* by Douglas Turner Ward, Copyright © 1966 by Douglas Turner Ward.

Theodore Ward for his scene from *The Daubers*, Copyright © 1953 by Theodore Ward.

CONTENTS

To those forgotten or unknown—who daily lead us
nearer freedom.

INTRODUCTION

African theatre played an important social and historical role. Men traveled from village to village telling stories and keeping the people informed of events going on in other towns and far away places. Musicians often accompanied the story teller who was also an expert at telling tales based upon legend and mythology; stories that pointed out a moral and usually used animals who thought and spoke as human beings. A man named Aesop used this method. He was said to have been an Ethiopian brought to Greece as a captive slave. Aesop's fables have been passed down to us, from five hundred years before the birth of Christ, to this day.

In many parts of Africa heat and humidity destroyed imported libraries of paper books. Records carved on wood were eaten by termites, and even houses did not endure for long periods of time. Africans, fortunately, were able to pass on information by word of mouth; in this way they were preserving the historical records of thousands of tribal groups. Each nation had actors, dancers and singers who were trained to perform messages from the past. They taught their pantomimes, speeches, dances, and songs to others who also pledged to keep them alive by passing knowledge and artistry on to the next generation. Historians say these performances have been faithfully duplicated for hundreds of years.

Those Africans who were defeated in battle and became victims of the slave trade, were abruptly cut off from their culture and suddenly placed in a strange, new and hostile environment. They began to create another culture based upon old memories and new conditions. This was difficult because slave traders sold them in mixed language groups to prevent communication. They were forbidden, by law, to use African languages, or to use drums because drums were traditional African message instruments. Although forbidden to speak any but the "master's" language it was at the same time against the law for them to learn to read and write the new tongue. At night, those in bondage, gathered around the campfire and sang the story of their troubles in sad new songs. Unable to write down these song stories, they passed them on to us by word of mouth; *Spirituals*, we call this music inspired by a life of hardship and sorrow. This form, along with Jazz, was the only new kind of music to spring from the new world called America.

In 1823 the free Blacks of New York City opened a theatre at what is now Bleecker and Grove Streets in Greenwich Village. James Hewlett, a West Indian, was the founder. The company performed Shakespearean drama. The white press and some of the public resented these Africans performing Richard III. A mob protested by pelting them with rocks. The company was arrested, jailed, and warned that in the future they must limit themselves to material more suitable to their station in life.

A few historians have named Ira Aldridge, great Shakespearean tragedian, as a member of The Grove Theatre Company. Aldridge went to Europe and there became famous and honored for acting the roles of Othello, King Lear, Macbeth, and Shylock.

In the early 1800s, in America, it was against the law for Black and white actors to perform together. Entertainers "of color" were confined to playing in tawdry bars and dives, places unadvertised and located off the beaten track. Many artists working in this environment were truly great and yet almost totally unknown to the general public. They were usually paid in tips alone and often depended on handouts for food and lodging. Because these places of criminal reputation were the only ones where the African-American entertainer could work, in time many people began to associate him with this kind of background and considered this to be "his place" where he "naturally" belonged.

William Wells Brown has been named as the first American Negro to write a play. Brown escaped from slavery and became a public speaker, novelist and playwright. One of his dramas was titled *The Escape* or *A Leap for Freedom*. This play was published in Boston in 1858, but never performed. Brown sometimes appeared at abolitionist meetings, with Frederick Douglass, and read from his work. Another play by Brown was *Experience* or *How to Give a Northern Man a Backbone*.

Often we have heard complaints about the one theme used most by Black writers, freedom. But seldom are writers of any race able to write outside of their own experience. Black experience means living a segregated and very special existence. There may be a few who were raised within a white experience and so are able to write best in this vein, but it is indeed rare.

In the last forty years there have been approximately eighteen plays by Black playwrights presented on Broadway. Two or three of these have been evaluated and re-evaluated in articles and books. It is obvious that this amount of work does not represent one fourth of a normal season's presentations on Broadway. Broadway is an important measure of a playwright's progress in the theatre, not because of the content or form of works done there, but because they are more regularly reviewed and become universally known.

There is yet little of our writing which reaches masses of people through television, radio, motion pictures or large-stage presentation. This lack has nothing to do with our capabilities. It is quite noticeable that most of what is produced in the professional theatre fails, and these failures have been accepted by critics, for over a century, as the price exacted for occasionally finding what eventually proves to be vital, worth-while and enduring drama.

Actors, directors and students of drama often ask for practice material to be used in classrooms or for audition purposes, scenes written by and about Black experience. The scenes in this book are a step toward that need. They were not selected as "the best" or "the first" of their kind, neither will they give you a cross-section of the works of all Black playwrights. I hope they will be useful to you and cause you to be more interested in the authors, and to seek others not in this collection. Some who are available in print are listed in the back of this book. These few scenes may inspire you to write your own. There's always room for another writer to pass on all that we possess from one generation to another.

ALICE CHILDRESS

BLACK SCENES

Scene from
PURLIE VICTORIOUS
by Ossie Davis

CHARACTERS

> PURLIE VICTORIOUS JUDSON
> LUTIEBELLE GUSSIE MAE JENKINS, his girl
> MISSY JUDSON, his sister
> GITLOW JUDSON, his brother-in-law
> IDELLA LANDY, neighbor

SCENE

> *The setting is the plain and simple interior of an antiquated, run-down farmhouse such as Negro sharecroppers still live in, in South Georgia. Threadbare but warm-hearted, shabby but clean.*
> PURLIE *tells* LUTIEBELLE, MISSY, *and* GITLOW *how he destroyed Cap'n Cotchipee.*

MISSY   How did you do it, Purlie?

LUTIEBELLE   What happened when you first got there?

PURLIE   (*Almost laughing*)   Now wait a minute—don't rush me!

MISSY   That's what I say: don't rush him—let the man talk!

PURLIE   Talk! Missy, I told you. I haven't got time—

GITLOW   That's all right, Purlie, we'll listen in a hurry.

LUTIEBELLE   What happened when you called him out and whipped him?

PURLIE   I didn't call him out and whip him!

GITLOW   What!

MISSY   You didn't!

LUTIEBELLE   Reb'n Purlie—?

PURLIE   I mean, I did call him out!

LUTIEBELLE   (*In ecstatic relief*)   Oh—you did call him out!

PURLIE   Yeah—but he didn't come.

ALL   What!

PURLIE   So—er—I went in to get him!

ALL   You did! Sure enough! What happened then?

PURLIE   (*Still seeking escape*)   Well, like I told you—

LUTIEBELLE   Tell us, Reb'n Purlie—please!

PURLIE   (*No escape*)   Well—here was me; and there was him—twisted and bent like a pretzel! Face twitchified like a pan of worms; eyes bugging out; sweat dreening down like rain; tongue plumb clove to the roof of his mouth! (*He looks to his audience, and is impelled to go on.*) Well—this thief! This murderer; this adulterer—this oppressor of all my people, just a sitting there: Stonewall Jackson Cotchipee, just a sitting there. (*Begins to respond to his own fantasy*) "Go to, rich

man, weep and howl, for your sorrows shall come upon you."
And-a "Wherefore abhor yourself, and repent Ye in sackcloth
and ashes!" cause ol' Purlie is done come to get you!

LUTIEBELLE (*Swept away*) Oh, my Lawd!

MISSY What he do, Purlie—what he do!?

PURLIE Fell down on bended knees and cried like a baby!

MISSY Ol' Cap'n Cotchipee on his knees!?

GITLOW Great day in the morning time!

PURLIE (*Warming to the task*) Don't beg me, white folks, it's
too late. "Mercy?" What do you know about mercy?! Did you
have mercy on Ol' Uncle Tubb when he asked you not to cheat
him out of his money so hard, and you knocked him deaf in
his left ear? Did you have mercy on Lolly's boy when he
sassed you back, and you took and dipped his head in a
bucket of syrup! And twenty years ago when little Purlie,
black and manly as he could be, stood naked before you
and your bull whip and pleaded with tears in his li'l ol' eyes,
did you have mercy?!

GITLOW Naw!

PURLIE —And I'll not have mercy now!

ALL Amen! Help him, Lawd! Preach it, boy, preach it! (*Etc.*)

PURLIE Vengeance is mine saith the Lord! (Hallelujah!) Ye
serpents; ye vipers; ye low-down sons of—! (Amen!) How
can ye escape the damnation of hell!

MISSY Throw it at him, boy!

PURLIE And then, bless my soul, I looked up—up from the
blazing depths of my righteous indignation! And I saw tears
spill over from his eyeballs; and I heard the heart beclutching
anguish of his outcry! His hands was both atremble; and
slobber adribblin' down his lips!

GITLOW Oh, my Lawd!

PURLIE And he whined and whimpered like a ol' hound dog
don't want you to kick him no more!

LUTIEBELLE Great goodness a mighty!

PURLIE And I commenced to ponder the meaning of this evil thing that groveled beneath my footstool—this no-good lump of nobody!—not fit to dwell on this earth beside the children of the blessed—an abomination to the Almighty and stench in the nostrils of his people! And yet—(*Pause for effect*) And yet—a man! A weak man; a scared man; a pitiful man; like the whole southland bogged down in sin and segregation crawling on his knees before my judgment seat—but still a MAN!

GITLOW A man, Lawd!

PURLIE He, too, like all the South, was one of God's creatures—

MISSY Yes, Lawd!

PURLIE He, too, like all the South, could never be beyond the reach of love, hope, and redemption.

LUTIEBELLE Amen!

PURLIE Somewhere for him—even for him, some father's heart was broken, some mother's tears undried.

GITLOW Dry 'em, Lawd!

PURLIE I am my brother's keeper!

ALL Yes, Lawd.

PURLIE And thinking on these things, I found myself to pause, and stumble in my great resolve—and sorrow squeezed all fury from my heart—and pity plucked all hatred from my soul —and the racing feet of an avenging anger slowed down to a halt and a standstill—and the big, black, and burly fist of my strong correction—raised on high like a stroke of God's own lightning—fell useless by my side. The book say, "Love one another."

MISSY Love one another!

PURLIE The book say, "Comfort ye one another."

LUTIEBELLE Comfort ye one another.

PURLIE The book say, "Forgive ye one another."

GITLOW   Forgive Ol' Cap'n, Lawd.

PURLIE   Slowly I turned away—to leave this lump of human mess and misery to the infinite darkness of a hell for white folks only, when suddenly—

MISSY   Suddenly, Lawd.

PURLIE   Suddenly I put on my brakes—Purlie Victorious Judson stopped dead in his tracks—and stood stark still, and planted his feet and rared back, asked himself and all the powers-that-be some mighty important questions.

LUTIEBELLE   Yes, he did, Lawd.

MISSY   And that is the truth!

PURLIE   How come—I asked myself—it's always the colored folks got to do all the forgiving?

GITLOW   Man, you mighty right!

PURLIE   How come the only cheek gits turned in this country is the Negro cheek!

MISSY   Preach to me, boy!

PURLIE   What was this, this—man—Ol' Cap'n Cotchipee—that in spite of all his sins and evils, he still had dominion over me?

LUTIEBELLE   Ain't that the truth!

PURLIE   God made us all equal—God made us all brothers—

ALL   Amen, amen.

PURLIE   "And hath made of one blood all nations of men for to dwell on the face of the earth."—Who changed all that?!

GITLOW   (*Furious*)   Who changed it, he said!

PURLIE   Who took it and twisted it around?!

MISSY   (*Furious*)   Who was it, he said!

LUTIEBELLE   (*Furious*)   And where's that scoun' hiding?!

PURLIE   So that the Declarator of Independence himself might seem to be a liar?

GITLOW Who, that's what I want to know, who?

PURLIE That a man the color of his face (*Pointing up Cotchipee Hill*) could live by the sweat of a man the color of mine!

LUTIEBELLE Work with him, Lawd, work with him!

PURLIE —Could live away up there in his fine, white mansion, and us down here in a shack not fitting to house the fleas upon his dogs!

GITLOW Nothing but fleas!

PURLIE —Could wax hisself fat on the fat of the land; steaks, rice, chicken, roastineers, sweet potato pies, hot buttered biscuits and cane syrup anytime he felt like it and never hit a lick at a snake! And us got to every day git-up-and-git-with-it, sunup-to-sundown, on fatback and cornmeal hoecakes—and don't wind up owning enough ground to get buried standing up in!

MISSY Do, Lawd!

PURLIE —And horses and Cadillacs, bull whips and bourbon, and two for 'leven dollar seegars—and our fine young men to serve at his table; and our fine young women to serve in his bed!

LUTIEBELLE Help him, Lawd.

PURLIE Who made it like this—who put the white man on top?

GITLOW That's what I wants to know!

PURLIE Surely not the Lord God of Israel who is a just God!

MISSY Hah, Lawd!

PURLIE And no respecter of persons! Who proved in the American Revolution that all men are created equal!

GITLOW Man, I was there when he proved it!

PURLIE Endowed with Civil Rights and First Class Citizenship, Ku Klux Klan, White Citizens Council notwithstanding!

MISSY Oh yes, he did!

PURLIE And when my mind commenced to commemorate and to reconsider all these things—

GITLOW Watch him, Lawd!

PURLIE And I thought of the black mother in bondage (Yes) and I thought of the black father in prison (Ha, Lawd!) And of Momma herself—Missy can tell how pretty she was—

MISSY Indeed I can!

PURLIE How she died outdoors on a dirty sheet cause the hospital doors said—"For white folks only." And of Papa, God rest his soul—who brought her tender loving body back home—and laid her to sleep in the graveyard—and cried himself to death among his children!

MISSY (*Crying*) Purlie, Purlie—

PURLIE (*Really carried away*) Then did the wrath of a righteous God possess me; and the strength of the host and of ten thousand swept into my good right arm—and I arose and I smote Ol' Cap'n a mighty blow! And the wind from my fist ripped the curtains from the eastern walls—and I felt the weight of his ol' bull whip nestling in my hands—and the fury of a good Gawd-almighty was within me; and I beat him—I whipped him—and I flogged him—and I cut him—I destroyed him! (IDELLA *enters.*)

GITLOW Great day and the righteous marching—whoeeeee! Man, I ain't been stirred that deep since the tree caught fire on a possum hunt and the dogs pushed Papa in the pot.

MISSY Idella, you shoulda heard him!

IDELLA I did hear him—all the way across the valley. I thought he was calling hogs. Well, anyway: all hell is broke loose at the big house. Purlie, you better get outta here. Ol' Cap'n is on the phone to the sheriff.

MISSY Ol' Cap'n Cotchipee is dead.

IDELLA The hell you preach.

ALL What!

IDELLA Ol' Cap'n ain't no more dead than I am.

LUTIEBELLE That's a mighty tacky thing to say about your ex-fellow man.

MISSY Mighty tacky.

LUTIEBELLE Reb'n Purlie just got through preaching 'bout it. How he marched up Cotchipee hill—

GITLOW (*Showing the bull whip*) And took Ol' Cap'n by the bull whip—

MISSY And beat that ol' buzzard to death!

IDELLA That is the biggest lie since the devil learned to talk!

LUTIEBELLE I am not leaving this room till somebody apologizes to Reb'n Purlie V. Judson, the gentleman of my intended.

IDELLA Purlie Judson! Are you gonna stand there sitting on your behind, and preach these people into believing you spent the night up at the big house whipping Ol' Cap'n to death when all the time you was breaking into the commissary!

GITLOW Something is rotten in the cotton!

PURLIE It's all right, Miz Idella—I'll take it from there—

MISSY It is not all right—!

PURLIE While it is true that, maybe, I did not go up that hill just word for word, and call that ol' man out, and beat him to death so much on the dotted line—!

MISSY (*Snatching up the paper bag*) I'm goin' to take back my lunch!

LUTIEBELLE You know what, Aunt Missy?

MISSY Yes, honey?

LUTIEBELLE Sometimes I just wish I could drop dead for a while!

PURLIE Wait, Lutiebelle, give me a chance to—

LUTIEBELLE Here's your money! (*Puts roll into* PURLIE's *hand*)

And that goes for every other great big ol' handsome man in the whole world!

PURLIE   What you want me to do? Go up that hill by myself and get my brains knocked out?

MISSY   It's little enough for the woman you love!

LUTIEBELLE   Why'd you have to preach all them wonderful things that wasn't so?

GITLOW   And why'd you have to go and change your mind?

PURLIE   I didn't mean for them not to be so: it was a—a parable! A prophecy! Believe me! I ain't never in all my life told a lie I didn't mean to make come true, some day!

✿   ✿   ✿

Scene from
TO KILL A DEVIL
by Roger Furman

CHARACTERS
>CARL, a teen-age boy
>His MOTHER

SCENE
>*Music is heard coming from a radio. The room is small and divided by a curtain. There is an armchair and a small table, a chest of drawers. Carl's* MOTHER *is sitting there fanning herself with a flashlight battery fan; dressed in a cheap housecoat. She is in her late thirties, becoming too plump for comfort. She drinks from a quart bottle of beer.*

CARL (*From kitchen*) Ma! Ma! (*Enters*) Can't you hear? I just offered to take you to the movies. Come on, Ma, Shelley Winters and bad Jim Brown . . .

MOTHER Maybe some other time . . . I can't tonight. Some other time, huh?

CARL (*Imploring*) I might not have the money some other time! Come on, be a sport.

MOTHER Not this evening. I have a very important date tonight.

CARL (*Crestfallen*) Yeah, I know.

MOTHER I just met a very nice man! (*Loud*) Yes I did! This man is really into something. He ain't no fool and you don't hear him talking that Black Power either. He got a real good job and a business on the side. This fool ain't got nothing but some money.

CARL You said the same thing last time. Mr. White, and the crazy Mr. Lee. Such nice gentlemen they were supposed to be.

MOTHER Not an ounce of brains between the two of them. What did they know? Like I said, this cat is into something. He's got his program together. (*Raising her voice*) I'm a grown woman, I know what I'm doing. It's no good for a person like me to be alone.

CARL Who's alone? I'm here, ain't I?

MOTHER Oh, what's the use of talking to a child. It hasn't been easy for me all these years raising you without a father's help. You're just a care-free kid, how would you know what I'm talking about. As long as you've got your three meals a day and a warm place to lay your head . . . life is just wonderful for you. If your father was with us things might have been a little better . . . for both of us.

CARL Is that why you had so many boy friends? When Buddy's

father died his mother never got married again. She's happy, ain't she?

MOTHER   Sure, she's married to that store-front church. Life is to be lived, not wasted beating a damn tambourine on some dirty street corner . . . talking about Christ is the answer. Getting me a good man is my answer.

CARL   You never talk about my father!

MOTHER   Carl, I look at you each day and see your father on your face. Your papa was quite a man. He could charm the birds out of the trees. Him and that damn guitar of his. Every time you saw him he would be humming or playing. Carl, to tell the bitter truth, your father wasn't wrapped too tight . . . but when you're young and in love like I was . . . things like that are very unimportant. We thought that life was just one big ball. We took a boat on down to the big city and got married. You was sure one boss baby. You were very pretty. Kinda dark though.

CARL   All right! Watch that stuff. Black is beautiful. (*They laugh.*)

MOTHER   He started running around. I wanted to be a good wife to him. It just didn't work! (*She moves downstage.* CARL *is sitting on the floor.*) One night . . . it was raining . . . the wind was blowing like it came straight from hell. It seemed like the whole world was wet. He walked in the door . . . stood there looking at me. (*Almost crying*) Like I had done him bad. I was holding you in my arms. He looked so strange all wet from the rain. He took your little hands and kissed them . . . ran his wet hand over my face and smiled to himself. He took his guitar down from the wall and walked out. Just like that it was all over. When my sister Ruby was coming here she begged me to come with her . . . I might get a new start. That new start never came. That's all in the past. This time it will work. I know it will.

CARL   (*Sharply*)   Maybe it's better like this!

MOTHER   (*Intense*)   No! It's not better.

CARL I worked all last summer, didn't I? I gave you some money to help with the rent. I can get another job. There are a lot of ways I can make money on the streets. I'm no fool.

MOTHER I'm not going to let Harlem kill you like it's killed so many others. I don't want to see you out there on those streets. I may not be what you think is the best mother in the world . . . I never turned my back on you. Thick or thin, I kept you.

CARL I know you did, Ma. You don't have to keep telling me what you did for me.

MOTHER (*Slightly straightening the room*) I just don't want you to forget it! No man has ever laid his hands on you either. Love me, love my child . . . I always say. (*Working up anger*) Living in broken-down apartments . . . no hot water! Evil people always messing with you . . . watching your youth go down the drain. Wondering, when I come home from work, if they'll tell me my child died from an overdose. I'm not that strong! I need a man to help me! I need a man that I can look up to and love. I don't even need the fine house . . . I don't need nothing. But I've got to feel that I'm loved.

CARL Ma, you know that I'll always love you . . . no matter what I might do or say.

MOTHER This is my last chance. Something always goes wrong, no matter how hard I try. If it wasn't for bad luck I wouldn't have any luck at all. Something good has to happen to me just once. I can't go on like this. Do you understand?

CARL I understand. I'll do anything I can to . . .

MOTHER I hope so! I really hope so. (*She goes into the next room, talks from behind curtain.*) Your aunt . . . the other day she told me that you never come to see her any more. Now that school is out . . . she thought that you would like to come stay with her for a while . . . no?

CARL No! I don't want to go there for even one day.

MOTHER (*Coming out with iron she plugs into light socket*)

Her kids are always asking for their cousin Carl. You spend so much of your time running around the street. You should be around your aunt and uncle. They will get you up on Sundays and make you go to church like you should.

CARL   Look Ma . . . I can't make that scene. A house full of babies, those cats running all over the place . . . and that big old smelly dog. Besides I'll have to sleep on the floor.

MOTHER   I wish to God I had a dime for every time I had to sleep on the floor. You don't know what a hard time is. You make me sick.

CARL   I don't see you going over there that much.

MOTHER   I just told you that I met a nice man.

CARL   I get it. You want to put me out.

MOTHER   (*Wearily*)   You said you wanted to see me happy. You know how some men are when they see a kid around the place. Please, Carl, don't make me beg you. (*Takes his hands*)

CARL   (*Shaking loose*)   I'll get up early and go out. I'll come in late. He won't even know I'm in the house. I can sleep on the fire escape . . . all right?

MOTHER   I'm getting older every day! You don't know what it is for a woman to be without some kind of husband. Try hard to understand! Baby, this man might be the one to save me from going crazy from loneliness. (*She hugs him.*) I know that you are here . . . I don't know what I'd do without you.

CARL   (*Turns away from her*)   That's why you want to put me out. You always wanted to get rid of me.

MOTHER   That's not true.

CARL   New boy friend! They never last! Aw, Ma, why don't you wise up?

MOTHER   It's not like I'm sending you to be with total strangers. Hell, Ruby is your own flesh and blood. (*She takes a sip of the beer, looks at him for a moment, places her hand on his shoulder.*) Carl, I've got your things all ready . . . packed in your room. All that you'll need. I will see that you have money to spend. Tell you what! I will get you that pretty pink suit you saw on 125th Street last week. With the shoes to match. How's that? (*Thinks he's considering the offer*) The way you kids are dressing nowadays. Red, blue, pink . . . I even saw a orange one trimmed in black . . . it was really something else.

CARL You packed all my things?

MOTHER (*Talking fast*) I might be able to squeeze out a extra pair of shoes . . . what you call them . . . gaters? (*Drinking some beer*) You really gonna have your program together. You're gonna be a real gone guy! (*Trying another approach*) God, please help my only child. God, look down and have mercy. Carl, Mama wants you to be the happiest boy in the whole world. (*Appeals to him*) I want to move out of here. This cat got some bread too, baby. If there is a God up there watching over us . . . then he better get himself together and throw some good luck our way. Don't spoil it, please don't spoil it for Mama.

CARL Ma, I don't want to leave.

MOTHER Oh, stop it. (*At the point of tears*) Look, it's getting late. He'll be here any moment to pick me up. (*She puts on her dress, starts to fix her face.*) How do I look? Zip me up like a good boy. You've still got your gang to run around with. It'll only be for a short time.

CARL They've got a thing on for tonight. They might even kill somebody. I don't wanta be with them no more.

MOTHER When I tell you something I want you to do it. I'm your mother and not one of those street friends of yours and don't you forget it!

CARL My mother! Don't think I don't know what goes on round here.

MOTHER (*Vexed*) You better have some respect! Don't you

ever talk to me like that! I went through too much for you! (*Screaming at him*) Get your things and get the hell over to my sister's house before I knock your silly head off. Boy, don't think you're too big for me to handle.

CARL   Drop dead! I hope you drop dead! Drop dead! I got a big thing on for tonight, . . . you're already dressed up for yours! Drop dead! (*He runs out of the house.*)

MOTHER (*Yells after him*)   Get out of my house! Get out!

CARL (*Off stage, in the distance*)   Drop dead! Drop dead!

MOTHER (*Astonished*)   Crazy kid. Talking to me like that. My whole life for that kid. That's the thanks I get. (*She starts to fix her face*) They don't understand a thing you try to do for them. It's no good for a woman like me to be alone. It's just no good.

*   *   *

Scene from
THE BIRD CAGE
by Floyd Barbour

CHARACTERS
   TAD, a Black boy in his late teens
   RHEA, a young Black woman

TIME
   Evening to dark of the present

SCENE
   Backyard porch of the Stokes's home in a small southern town. Right is a tree whose branches stretch out over the yard and whose limbs support a swing. Piano music can be heard coming faintly from the house.

RHEA (*Wearing a colorful housedress. She comes to the screen door and looks out. Wipes her hands on her apron. Pushes open door and comes out onto porch.*) Ta-ad! Ta-ad! (*Looks up in tree, then calls back over her shoulder*) It's all right, Miss Maude, he was up in the tree all the time. (*To* TAD . . . *as piano music starts again*) We been callin' and callin' you. (TAD *jumps out of tree . . . holding bird cage, hangs it onto lower branch.*)

TAD Maybe he'll come back . . . or maybe he's dead. Leave anything around here and it dies.

RHEA He didn't die. He only flew away.

TAD Through the bars?

RHEA When they fly off like that . . . they fly off.

TAD Where?

RHEA I don't know, Tad. You never said a word about your vacation. You ain't even said a word about Lark. How he is or nothin'. And your father. You ain't even asked about Lolly.

TAD I've only had time to catch my breath and fetch this cage which is empty and which once contained my bird.

RHEA Lolly's been over here almost every day askin' when you were comin' back.

TAD . . . huh, I don't want to see her.

RHEA (*Musing*) Green County. I ain't been there in a month of Sundays. Then it was because Buster took me.

TAD It's just a place. What did Lolly want?

RHEA To see you, I suppose.

TAD All she ever talks about is the African Salvation of God Church!

RHEA A little salvation might do you some good.

TAD   Then, where is it? Where is African Salvation? (*Gives a couple of birdcalls to the lost bird*)

RHEA   (*Pouring glasses of lemonade*) Miss Maude says you don't have to read to her tonight.

TAD   Good. I'm tired of Negro History. (*He takes glass of lemonade and raises it.*) A toast. To things we love. (*She touches her glass to his.*)

RHEA   To things we love.

TAD   When I die, I want carved on my stone: That was not what I meant, that was not it at all . . .

RHEA   (*Examining a pair of dark glasses*) Them your dark glasses I found?

TAD   In Green County, Lark has a pair just like them. Wears them day and night. Says they put a screen between him and life. Lark would want to know what she means by African Salvation. He would just want to know. That Lolly.

RHEA   For somebody we don't want to see, we sure are busy talkin' about her.

TAD   Lark's pretty important in Green County.

RHEA   I'm sure he is.

TAD   You ever drag race? How come you never liked him?

RHEA   Who?

TAD   Lark.

RHEA   I like him, Tad. I'm just always wonderin' what's goin' to become of him. Black boys like him get into trouble.

TAD   Some people go places, some people break the sound barrier. We can't even break the silence . . .

RHEA   I don't know . . .

TAD   That's your trouble: You'll never know! (*After a silence.*) Thought Buster was coming.

RHEA Buster done gone off. (*Takes harmonica out of her pocket*) He left you this. I polished it.

TAD I'm going to miss Buster.

RHEA I was always afraid he'd do somethin' and—trouble. Walkin' along the road and all of a sudden he'd throw out his arms like this and let out a yell. Buster standin' in the road with his arms thrown out, sayin' that somethin' was inside him, somethin' Black was inside him and had to be let out!

TAD You miss him.

RHEA Sure I do. I miss you, don't I, when you gone only a short while. Buster and me be together goin on two years—on and off.

TAD Lark says it's the white folks who've done it.

RHEA He may have somethin there.

TAD He says they've locked us in . . . and I go along with him.

RHEA Maybe you're 'bove me.

TAD No, I'm not. You're alive. You breathe in southern air. . . . They let my bird out.

RHEA You locked him in.

TAD My bird. (*Quiet. He plays a familiar tune on the harmonica. Moves out into the yard. Stops playing.*) Lark says there was a time when a week didn't pass without a funeral—violent death. One of these funerals was his father's. His father was a delivery boy. Used to deliver lunches. One hot noon some white men decided to have some fun. They had "Old Shorty" deliver a large order to them at the plant: hamburgers, bologna, and cheese sandwiches . . . so many to the top floor and so many to the first floor. Soon as "Old Shorty" got to the top floor, someone on the first floor would call him. Soon as he got to the first, someone on the top would call him; Hey, coon, nigger, shine, hey—! The whole place was shaking with laughter, seeing "Old Shorty" run; laughter is catching. He died on the second landing. His heart gave out, just stopped. It was such a pitiful funeral, Lark says, one single wreath of flowers. From the men at the plant. He felt sad because his father hadn't even left them a memory of having done something that was *his* something.

(*Quiet*)

Buster written to you?

RHEA   No, Buster don't write. I'm not you, you know: moanin and groanin if you don't get a postcard. Buster thinks of me.

TAD   How do you know?

RHEA   Well, I think of Buster. Maybe that's enough.

TAD   I'll be here next summer and the summer after that. I'll be playing this harmonica and you'll be sitting in that swing. Right here. Look at this cage. I fixed it, polished it, hung it . . . for what! I thought that bird needed me . . . Just goes to show you; caring about things that can't stand us. Just goes to show you.

RHEA   Tad, if you leave that cage in the tree, who knows? Bird yellow might just find it. He's probably just tryin his wings.

TAD   They go off. But we don't, and if we do, we come right back, sure as clockwork. (*Sounds of the evening. Pause.*) Rhea, I let Lark down this summer. I let him down. He wanted me to join him. I didn't. A white man came from the North . . . this summer, with books and charts, saying he was trying to raise the standard of understanding in the South. He was a young, white man right out of college. He lived on the edge of the Black district. Lark wanted us to break into his place and tear up all he had. Lark said he's seen too many like him. They come from all over, into the Black district, take what they can from us, and move back to where they come from. They come under the pretense of doing good for black people. Actually, they're just white, and they want to make a living off our misery and our music.

RHEA   That's the truth.

TAD   Lark's family has been on State Aid since his father died.

He says he's seen his things taken from him too many times.
He says he hates them and waits for the day of Black revenge
. . . when he'll go into the white section, take what they have,
and leave a bloody trail behind him; and he'll do it too. Says
he can't wait for that day, and that day is surely coming!

RHEA   Yes, Lawd. And what's goin' to happen on that day?

TAD   White flesh is going to melt from white bones. White minds
are going to leave white bodies. And all the streets are going
to be named after us: Billie Holiday Place and Father Divine
Boulevard and Malcolm X Road . . . And our dead will come
back, stepping along the road . . . all our dead; the slave dead,
the hunted . . . dead . . . the alcohol dead, the lynched dead,
the convict dead, the dope dead, the wine dead, the cheated
dead, the scared dead, the gone, forgotten dead . . . and the
earth will rumble with the sound of that army.—Sure as
licorice is black, as Lark says.

RHEA   I hear what Lark say, what do you say?

TAD   I go along with him, but I couldn't see tearing up this
white man's books. Nor could I see any reason for *not* doing it.
It just wasn't what I would feel right about. I told Lark this.
He called me a Booker T. Said I was afraid of the man. Said
he wasn't afraid of nothing. Says he goes anywhere he wants
to, anybody says anything to him, gets it! —But I couldn't
feel right about it. For myself. So I let him down. . . . But
I think everyone has to find his own way of doing things.

RHEA   And your way?

TAD   Maybe teaching. I'd like to do something before night
closes in—

RHEA   You will.

TAD   I don't know. I think Lark's got something: I don't think the
white world is going to let any of us do any of the things we
want to do.

RHEA   (*Rising*) (*Sighs deeply*)   Summer's almost over.

TAD   Some summers don't end. We haven't seen the last of it.

It will slip into fall, and winter will become mixed with it, then spring. And there will be no place for spring to carry us—except into summer—and we're already into it—(TAD *is inspecting the bird cage.* RHEA *strikes a match.*)

RHEA How long you think it takes this light to reach one of them stars?

TAD Millions, millions of years. Where's the tool box? I want to fix this.

RHEA Round the side of the house. (TAD *goes off left.* RHEA *sits in the swing for a while.*) Millions and millions of years. (*Comes downstage*) Hear that, Buster? Millions of years. And where are you tonight? Tad was playin' that tune tonight. Minded me so much of you. You tellin' me that as long as you was around I had nothin' to worry about. I guess the main thing is that it gets played. Gets loose in the world. . . . Oh, Buster, I wish you were here tonight. Standin next to me. Holdin my hand. Oh, Buster. I do miss you. Your touch . . . your sweet touch . . . and your laughter. (RHEA *is crossing back to porch as* TAD *returns with pliers to fix the cage.*)

TAD You talking to me?

RHEA No, just talkin to the night. (*Standing on the porch*) I was thinkin . . . it don't matter so much whether affection comes back the way it goes out or not. As long as it goes out. . . . Good night, Tad.

TAD Good night, Rhea.

*   *   *

Scene from
SHOES
by Ted Shine

CHARACTERS

TRAVIS, a bus boy; fifteen

SMOKEY (Ronald), another bus boy; fourteen

MARSHALL, a semi-retarded cripple; he is also a bus boy;
fourteen

MR. WISELY, a waiter; middle-aged

SCENE

*A dingy storage room at a fashionable country club in Dallas.
Mr. Mack enters—an elderly waiter dressed in waiter's jacket
and formal trousers—sits talking to the boys.* TRAVIS, *a fif-
teen-year-old bus boy, is dressed in orange—shirt, slacks,
and shoes—a bright orange.* RONALD, *or* SMOKEY *as he is
called by the boys, is fourteen. He is dressed in a pale blue
and black outfit. The boys smoke restlessly.*

WISELY (*Moving down the stairs*) 'Evenin', boys!

SMOKEY I didn't think you was never gon' get here, Mr. Wisely. You bring my money?

WISELY Yeah, son, I got it. One hundred and fifty dollars in cash. That's a lot of money for a boy like you to be carrying around. You take it home and put it somewhere safe. Keep it for a rainy day. You ain't aimin' to spend it is you, son? I thought this was your school money.

SMOKEY Well . . . I . . . er . . .

TRAVIS It's already spent, Mr. Wisely.

WISELY What you spend it on, Ronald?

SMOKEY I got some shoes for school.

WISELY Oh. I see.

TRAVIS And two Pierre Cardin shirts and ties.

WISELY You been buying clothes all summer. You got enough to get you through this school year. Get them shoes and hang on to this money. Lots of little thing you may need once you back in school.

TRAVIS When he git them shoes ain't gon' be none left.

WISELY This boy's got sense. He was smart enough to put him some money aside from his check. He worked hard for this money and he ain't gonna throw it away just because he seen somethin' in a winda he liked. Ronald got sense.

MARSHALL Um-huh. That's what you think!

SMOKEY Can I have that money now, Mr. Wisely?

WISELY Sure, son. How much of it you plannin' to spend?

TRAVIS All of it! Them is eight-five dollar alligator shoes he's gettin', and them shirts is fifteen dollars apiece, and them two ties cost twenty dollars. That's . . . eight-five ninety-five—a hundred and fifteen dollars.

WISELY   This boy is lyin' ain't he, son?

SMOKEY   Yeah. I paid ten dollars on them shoes, so they ain't but seventy-five dollars! And I put five dollars on them shirts and ties, so they ain't but forty-five dollars!

WISELY   Rich folks don't spend that kinda money on clothes! You gone crazy? You a high school boy—a child! You wait till you get outta school, and get a real job, then you buy them kinda clothes if you got to have 'em. You could take this money and help your poor mama with it like Marshall here do. Don't just go waste it away.

SMOKEY   My mama work. She buy what she want. She know I'm gettin' these clothes and she say she was proud of me 'cause I know what quality is. She say if you buy somethin' good it-a last you. Now give me my money so I can get downtown before the store close.

WISELY   Didn't you sit right in here and tell me when you started to work that when you went back to school you was gonna make sure that it wasn't like last year? Didn't you tell me how you'd go without breakfast and lunch and sometimes without dinner 'cause your mama wouldn't be home and there wasn't no food or money in the house? Ain't that why you started savin' part of your check? So you could take care of yourself?

SMOKEY   I'm spending my money on me! I'm spendin' it on somethin' I can see and hold and know I got! I need them clothes, Mr. Wisely.

WISELY   I ain't sayin' you don't need them, son. What I'm sayin' is don't spend all your money on somethin' you can't afford. What would I look like tryin' to buy a yacht when I have to ride the bus to work?

SMOKEY   I say if you want a yatch you oughta try to get one.

MARSHALL   I seen mens buy Cadillacs what ain't got no place to stay, uh-huh.

SMOKEY   That's they business!

WISELY Yeah, 'cause they old fools and can't nobody tell 'em nothin'. Don't you be no young fool.

SMOKEY I know what I'm doin', Mr. Wisely. Mama say we ain't never had nothin' and ain't never gon' have nothin', so we better get what we can while we young and try to be happy, 'cause when you get old, life is hell.

WISELY Your life is hell right now, boy, and you too blind to see it. And if you continue listening to your mama it's gonna *be* hell!

SMOKEY That's all right, too.

WISELY What kinda example is she for you? She works six days a week and what she do with her money? Spend it upon pretty clothes like she a teen-ager, and hang out in them taverns every night of the week. How many times you seen her she ain't been drunk? You listen to a person like that? You got sense.

SMOKEY You just don't understand.

WISELY What don't I understand?

SMOKEY Mama may drank, but she ain't drunk that much. She say she have too 'cause of the way life is. She say if she had to face the world every day sober, she'd go crazy. She say them people she work for is enough to drive a person to drink.

MARSHALL Um-huh, then she ought quit!

TRAVIS Naw, man, when you work for white folks you got to break 'em just like you break in a horse. Mama say you got to get control over 'em and let 'em know you mean business. That takes *time*, baby, and it ain't easy. That's how come a maid what's done been with a family a long time don't quit —she done broke that family in—and she can go 'bout her business and do what she want to do 'cause they ain't gonna say nothin'.

SMOKEY You don't need to be hard on my mama. She do the best she can.

WISELY   Do she? Marshall's mama got eight children, but she work and feeds 'em, and she still find time to try to raise 'em right. Your mama just got you—and you's left to grow up in the wilderness like a weed. You think she really cares about you?

SMOKEY   You just don't understand, Mr. Wisely. Now gimme my money.

TRAVIS   Yeah. It's gettin' late and if we miss the next bus—

WISELY   I know this is your money, son, and I know what I'm doin' now may hurt you, but I'm gonna hold onto this money for a few more days.

SMOKEY   What??!!

WISELY   I'm gonna keep it till Monday. You go on home and think about what I done said, and if you still want to waste it up, I'll give it to you, but I don't want you doin' nothin' you'll be sorry for.

SMOKEY   I want my money *now*, Mr. Wisely!

WISELY   I know, son. I know how you feel. You got you' mind on something and you want to do it here and now. That's how the young mind works. I sits at home sometimes and watches the television and I see all them new cars being advertised. I wants one so bad I can taste it. I can feel myself sittin' behind the wheel of a Lincoln Continental. I can see myself driving down the streets and all the folk's eyes is starin' at me. I want that car so bad I almos' cry, but then I say, "Man, folks all over the world wants something. Some folks just want somethin' to eat or a roof over they head. Some folks just wants a job so they can take care of they family." Then I say, "If I had me that Lincoln, it would get old to me in a few months and I'd want somethin' else. Suppose somebody was to run into that seven-thousand-dollar car and didn't have no insurance?" I'd be mad and not satisfied. That's the circle of things, son. And the worst thing in a person's life is to be in debt. Don't be beholdin' to nobody. Have you some money put aside for yo'self. Suppose your mama got sick this winna and couldn't work? Suppose you got sick? You need somethin' somewhere to fall back on.

SMOKEY I want my money, *now, Mr. Wisely!*

WISELY You done trusted me, Ronald, for three months to hold this money. You can trust me two more days. You come by here—or I'll brang it to your house Monday.

MARSHALL He right, Smokey, man. You oughta think about it.

SMOKEY This is the las' day of my layaway! If I don't get it out today they go back in stock and I'm outta fifteen dollars!

WISELY I'd rather be outta fifteen dollars than a hundred and fifty.

TRAVIS Them shoes mean somethin' to him, Mr. Wisely.

WISELY Then get some cheaper ones! I make four times the money yawl makes and I ain't never wanted me no eighty-five dollar shoes! I ain't never wanted none 'cause I couldn't never afford none.

SMOKEY Can't nobody never afford nothin' to hear yawl tell it! That's all I heard all my life! When my ol' man and mama was together I'd ask him for an ice cream cone and he say he can't afford it. I wanted to go to the Fair once. I told him all summer that I wanted to go and I wanted him to take me. I say, "Daddy, save five dollars for us to spend." He say, "Okay!" I kept tellin' him all summer, and he kept sayin' okay. Come Fair time in October he say he couldn't go! I ask him for the money so I could go and he say he couldn't afford it! That very week he bought a car! I asked Mama for a Timex watch one Christmas. She give me a Christmas card and a pair of socks. She say she couldn't afford no watch, but she gave a party that night at the Empire Grill for her friends—they was drankin' good scotch on *her!* She had two seven-dollar fifths—yet she couldn't afford to buy me a nine dollar Timex watch! I got me this job this summer and I worked hard and saved my monty to buy me what I want. What*ever* I want!

TRAVIS Cool it, baby! Don't cry!

SMOKEY I ain't goin' to school raggady no more! Ain't nobody gon' laugh at me no more 'cause I got to wear tennis in the snow!

WISELY   Folks don't laugh at you, son, 'cause they don't like you. They laugh 'cause they in the same boat you's in and they don't want to admit it.

SMOKEY   School don't mean nothin' to me nohow, and if I can't be clean, I sho wouldn't go!

WISELY   You got to get yo' education!

SMOKEY   Why?

WISELY   So you can better yo'self.

SMOKEY   You say you went to high school! You don't need to go to high school to be no waiter!

WISELY   When I was yo' age that's about all there was around here for us to do—except maybe work at the post office—and you just about needed a college degree to get a job there! You can work almost anyplace today if you got a high school education. You can work at a bank or in some office building. And remember—it ain't what's on your back that folk's respect —it's what's in your haid! You act like you want to look better than yo' teachers.

SMOKEY   I'm *gonna* look better than they look!! Now give me my money, Mr. Wisely.

WISELY   Can't I reason with you none?

SMOKEY   No, sir! I want my money so I can get my things!

WISELY   What did I tell you, Ronald? Monday I'll . . .

SMOKEY   I want it now, Mr. Wisely! Monday I want to wear my outfit to school—*all* of it!

WISELY   Don't they teach you no sense a-tall at school?

SMOKEY   Give me my money!!!

WISELY   Son, ain't no use yellin' and carryin' on like a wild man—

TRAVIS   That bus gonna be here in a minute.

MARSHALL   If Mr. Roth don't let us work this winna, you could buy yo'self somethin' for Christmas wif that money. Uh huh, you could buy yo' mama a present!

SMOKEY   Mr. Wisely, you better give me my money now!

WISELY   Look at this boy!

SMOKEY   I ain't playin'!

WISELY   What did I tell you, Ronald! (*He starts to exit.* RONALD *grabs* MARSHALL's *gun and points it at* WISELY.)

SMOKEY   GIVE ME MY MONEY!

TRAVIS   Smokey, man!!

MARSHALL   Say, man, give me my gun!

WISELY   Where did you get that gun, boy?

TRAVIS   It's Marshall's—he bought it!

WISELY   You put that thing down!

SMOKEY   I ain't playin' with you, Mr. Wisely!

WISELY   Put that thing down, Ronald! You got no business with no gun—none of you! You just get yo'self into a whole heap of trouble over nothin'. You ain't the kinda kids to carry on like this. I'm surprised at you, Marshall. What's your mama gonna think when she finds out you done gone and bought yo'self a gun? You know better than this, Ronald—you all do! You got no business wif no gun, now you give it to me!

SMOKEY   Don't you get near me!

TRAVIS   Leave him alone, Mr. Wisely!

WISELY   This boy got sense. I been known' this boy since he was a baby. I been almost like a daddy to him. He got sense! Now you give me that gun, Ronald.

SMOKEY   You give me my money!!

WISELY   Put that gun down then.

SMOKEY   My money! And stop movin' in on me like that, Mr. Wisely!

WISELY Put it down, Ronald.

SMOKEY Stay over there!

WISELY I'm not gonna hurt you, son—

SMOKEY I know you ain't! Now give me my money!

TRAVIS Smokey!

MARSHALL Give me my gun, man!

SMOKEY I'm astin' you one more time for my money!

TRAVIS For God's sake, Mr. Wisely, give it to him!

WISELY This boy's got sense. He ain't gonna hurt ol' man Wisely, is ya?

MARSHALL He done gone crazy!

SMOKEY Keep away from me! (WISELY *continues to move slowly forward.*)

WISELY It's all right, son. Everything's all right. Put it down, now . . . come on (SMOKEY *closes his eyes and aims the gun directly at* WISELY. MARSHALL *knocks the gun out of* SMOKEY's *hand.*)

SMOKEY Lea' me alone! (WISELY *grabs* SMOKEY.)

WISELY Calm down, boy! I never thought I'd live to see the day *you'd* draw a pistol on me. Ain't I been yo' friend? Ain't I tried to treat you like a son-a-mine? Ain't me and my wife fed you? Bought you clothes when you didn't have none? Ain't I tried to be a good friend to you, boy? How come you want to treat me this way?

TRAVIS He didn't mean it, Mr. Wisely.

WISELY I seen this boy's eyes! He meant it! Well, Ronald, you don't have to worry about me no more.

MARSHALL You gon' call the police?

WISELY No, but you give me that gun.

MARSHALL What you gon' do with it? (*Gives him the gun*)

WISELY Get rid of it before one of yawl gits yo'selves in trouble. (*He removes his billfold and takes out the boy's money.*) You think I didn't have you money, son? You think I'd try to steal it or spend it or cheat you out of it? Here it is—all of it. One hundred and fifty dollars—cash. (*Forces the money into* SMOKEY's *hand*) Burn it up for all I care, but don't come 'round me no more. (*Pause as* WISELY *turns and starts up the stairs*)

SMOKEY Mr. Wisely . . . ? (WISELY *stops.*) This is my money and you oughta give it to me when I asted! (WISELY *walks over to the boy and slaps him, then turns and exits.*)

❀   ❀   ❀

Scene from
A SON COME HOME
by Ed Bullins

A boy who practically has had to raise himself, now seeks to piece together some of his past. He finds his mother living with members of a religious cult.

CHARACTERS
A MOTHER
Her SON

SCENE
Bare stage but for two chairs. MOTHER *enters and begins to use imaginary iron and ironing board. She hums a spiritual as she works. The* SON *follows her into the room.*

MOTHER You came three times . . . Michael? It took you three times to find me home?

SON Yes, home . . . an anachronism.

MOTHER What did you say, Michael?

SON Anachronism: One: an error in chronology; *esp:* a chronological misplacing of persons, events, objects, or customs in regard to each other. Two: a person or thing that is chronologically out of place . . . anachronistic/ *also* anachronic/ *or* anachronous—anachronistically also anachronously.

MOTHER I was so glad to hear you were going to school in California. I prayed for you.

SON Thank you.

MOTHER Thank the Lord, Michael. Are you still writing that radical stuff, Michael?

SON Radical?

MOTHER Yes . . . that stuff you write and send me all the time in those little books.

SON My poetry, Mother?

MOTHER Yes, that's what I'm talking about.

SON No.

MOTHER Praise the Lord, son. Praise the Lord. Didn't seem like anything I had read in school.

SON I've only seen my father about half a dozen times that I remember, Mother. What was he like?

MOTHER Down in the "Bottom" . . . that's where I met your father. I was young and hinkty then. Had big pretty brown legs and a small waist. Everybody used to call me Bernie . . . and me and my sister would go to Atlantic City on the weekends and work as waitresses in the evenings and sit all afternoon on the black part of the beach at Boardwalk and

Atlantic . . . getting blacker . . . and having the time of our lives. Your father probably still lives down in the bottom . . . perched over some bar down there . . . drunk to the world . . . I can see him now . . . he had good white teeth then . . . not how they turned later when he started in drinkin' that wine and wouldn't stop . . . he was so nice then. (*She paces up and down.*) I can be a witness to the retribution that's handed down. A witness to all that He'll bestow upon your sinner's head . . . A witness! . . . That's what I am Andy! Andy! Do you hear me? . . . A witness!

SON   Mother . . . what's wrong? What's the matter?

MOTHER   Thank the Lord that I am not blinded and will see the fulfillment of divine . . .

SON   Mother!

MOTHER   Oh . . . is something wrong, Michael?

SON   You're shouting and walking around.

MOTHER   Oh . . . it's nothing, son. I'm just feeling the power of the Lord.

SON   Oh . . . is there anything I can get you, Mother?

MOTHER   No, nothing at all. (*She sits again and irons.*)

SON   Where's your kitchen . . . I'll get you some coffee . . . the way you like it. I bet I still remember how to fix it.

MOTHER   Michael, I don't drink anything like that no more.

SON   No?

MOTHER   Not since I joined the service of the Lord.

SON   Yeah? . . . Well, do you mind if I get myself a cup?

MOTHER   Why, I don't have a kitchen. All my meals are prepared for me.

SON   Oh . . . I thought I was having dinner with you.

MOTHER   No. There's nothing like that here.

SON   Well, could I take you out to a restaurant? . . . Remember how we used to go out all the time and eat? I've never lost my habit of liking to eat out. Remember . . . we used to come down to this part of town and go to restaurants. They used to call it home cooking then . . . now, at least where I been out West and up in Harlem . . . we call it Soul Food. I bet we could find a nice little restaurant not four blocks from here, Mother. Remember that old man's place we used to go to on Nineteenth and South? I bet he's dead now . . . but . . .

MOTHER   I don't ever eat out no more, Michael.

SON   No?

MOTHER   Sometimes I take a piece of holy bread to work . . . or some fruit . . . if it's been blessed by my Spiritual Mother.

SON   I see.

MOTHER   Besides . . . we have a prayer meeting tonight.

SON   On Friday?

MOTHER   Every night. You'll have to be going soon.

SON   Oh.

MOTHER   You're looking well.

SON   Thank you.

MOTHER   But you look tired.

SON   Do I?

MOTHER   Yes, those rings around your eyes might never leave. Your father had them.

SON   Did he?

MOTHER   Yes . . . and cowlicks . . . deep cowlicks on each side of his head.

SON   Yes . . . I remember.

MOTHER   You do?

SON   How is Will, Mother?

MOTHER   I don't know . . . haven't seen your stepfather in years.

SON   Mother?

MOTHER   Yes, Michael.

SON   Why you and Will never got married? . . . You stayed together for over ten years.

MOTHER   Oh, don't ask me questions like that, Michael.

SON   But, why not?

MOTHER   It's just none of your business.

SON   But you could be married now . . . . not alone in this room . . .

MOTHER   Will had a wife and child in Chester . . . you know that.

SON   He could have gotten a divorce, Mother . . . why . . .

MOTHER   Because he just didn't . . . that's why.

SON   You never hear from him?

MOTHER   Last I heard . . . Will had cancer.

SON   Oh, he did.

MOTHER   Yes.

SON   Why didn't you tell me? . . . You could have written.

MOTHER   Why?

SON   So I could have known.

MOTHER   So you could have known? Why?

SON   Because Will was like a father to me . . . the only one I've really known.

MOTHER   A father? And you chased him away as soon as you got big enough.

SON   Don't say that, Mother.

MOTHER   You made me choose between you and Will.

SON   Mother.

MOTHER   The quarrels you had with him . . . the mean tricks you used to play . . . the lies you told to your friends about Will . . . He wasn't much . . . when I thought I had a sense of humor I usta call him just plain Will. But we was his family.

SON   Mother, listen.

MOTHER   And you drove him away . . . and he didn't lift a hand to stop you.

SON   Listen, Mother.

MOTHER   As soon as you were big enough you did all that you could to get me and Will separated.

SON   Listen.

MOTHER   All right, Michael . . . I'm listening. (*Pause*)

SON   Nothing (*The* SON *lifts an imaginary object.*) Is this your tambourine?

MOTHER   Yes.

SON   Do you play it?

MOTHER   Yes.

SON   Well?

MOTHER   Everything I do in the service of the Lord I do as well as he allows.

SON   You play it at your meetings.

MOTHER   Yes, I do. We celebrate the life He has bestowed upon us.

SON   I guess that's where I get it from.

MOTHER   Did you say something, Michael?

SON   Yes. My musical ability.

MOTHER   Oh . . . you've begun taking your piano lessons again?

SON   No . . . I was never any good at that.

MOTHER Yes, three different teachers and you never got past the tenth lesson.

SON You have a good memory, Mother.

MOTHER Sometimes, son. Sometimes.

SON I play an electric guitar in a combo.

MOTHER You do? That's nice.

SON That's why I'm in New York. We got a good break and came East.

MOTHER That's nice, Michael.

SON I was thinking that Sunday I could rent a car and come down and get you and drive you up to see our show. You'll get back in plenty of time to rest for work Monday.

MOTHER No, I'm sorry. I can't do that.

SON But you would like it, Mother. We could have dinner up in Harlem then go down and . . .

MOTHER I don't do anything like that any more, Michael.

SON You mean you wouldn't come to see me play even if I were appearing here in Philly?

MOTHER That's right, Michael. I wouldn't come. I'm past all that.

SON Oh, I see.

MOTHER Yes, thank the Lord.

SON But it's my life, Mother.

MOTHER Good . . . then you have something to live for.

SON Yes.

MOTHER Well, you're a man now, Michael . . . I can no longer live it for you. Do the best with what you have.

SON Yes . . . yes, I will, Mother.

OFF-STAGE VOICE Sister Brown! . . . Sister Brown . . . Bernice!

SON   I guess I better be going, Mother.

MOTHER   Yes.

SON   I'll write.

MOTHER   Please do.

SON   I will.

MOTHER   You're looking well . . . Thank the Lord.

SON   Thank you, so are you, Mother.

MOTHER   Take care of yourself, son.

SON   Yes, Mother, I will.

BLACKNESS

Scene from
A STREAK O' LEAN
by Abbey Lincoln

CHARACTERS

  J. D. LITTLE
  SARAH LITTLE, his wife

TIME Now

SCENE

  The front room of a house which is the kitchen, has a comfortable, lived-in appearance. There is an oblong wooden table with four mismatching chairs. Two face downstage, each at the opposite ends of the table. Stage left is a built-in long tool chest, which opens from the top. A curtained entrance is upstage, and to the right.

  A woman, forty, slightly built, wearing a housedress, is seated at the table, crocheting jewelry. Little boxes of beads and gold and silver spools of twine are on the table. On the tool chest is a display board with finished rings, bracelets, and headbands. A man, forty-five and vigorous, enters cautiously. He is carrying a small metal case and under his arm is a bag wrapped in his topcoat. The woman glances up and continues her work. He sets the metal case on the floor, locks and bolts the door, quickly looks out the window, pulls the shade, walks toward the woman, unwrapping the coat from the bag, throws the coat over a chair, and sets the bag on the table. Part of the beads, etc. fall to the floor.

SARA (*Gathering her paraphernalia*) One of these days I'll have my own place to work in, an' I dare you to set foot in it!

J.D. (*Undoes the string, opens the bag and stares in amazement.*) Honey, you mus' be sendin' up some hellova prayers!

SARAH (*Picking the beads from the floor*) I paid twenty cents a piece for these beads an' they don't even import 'em no more.

J.D. Sarah we rich! I jus' foun' a half a million dollars! Mus' be that much at least! (*He turns the bag up and money in wrappers spills over the table and onto the floor. He laughs joyously.*)

SARAH (*Covers her mouth to stop a scream. She reaches for a packet of money from the floor, examines it, and suddenly throws it down, stepping away.*) What chu doin' now?

J.D. (*Checking the money from his pocket*) Can't be no dream, cause the taxi was five dollars.

SARAH You havin' another one of those headaches? . . . How'd you come by all this . . .

J.D. (*Crawling along the floor, picking up the money*) Money! Money! Money!

SARAH (*She barricades the door with a chair.*)

J.D. Throw it all back in the bag. I gotta find Snake. (*At the phone, dialing*)

SARAH What's he got chu doin'? . . . Robbin' somebody?

J.D. Wait till I tell you about it . . . You know that short cut I use sometime comin' home from Juke's joint? That alley way in between Wilson an' . . . Damn, what's the name of that other street?

SARAH (*Impatiently*) I know what cha mean. Hubert! . . . Hubert Street!

J.D. (*Hanging the phone*) Where is everybody? Watch everything Sarah, I need the phone book. (*He races through the curtain.*)

SARAH (*As if in a trance, she walks to the table and stands, staring at the money.*)   Lord, now I know what his mother was talkin' about. (*She examines the bag, and leans weakly against the table.* J.D. *enters, carrying a medium-sized leatherbound notebook.*)

SARAH   You get this mess outta my house!

J.D.   Everything's all right. I'll tell you about it as soon as I find Snake. Get me a drink. (*A woman's wild laughter is heard off stage.* J.D. *dials a number.*)

SARAH   That's jus' where I'm gonna wind up one a these days, in the crazy house. If you don't get this mess outta here I'm gonna call the police!

J.D. (*Carefully, hanging the receiver*)   We been livin' together twenty years now, Sarah. You figure I went out an' robbed a bank?

SARAH   No!

J.D.   How you think I got it then?

SARAH (*High-pitched*)   I don't know, that's what I'm askin' you!

J.D.   You see this money all over the place, don't chu start screamin' in here! (*Wild laughter off stage*)

SARAH   Well, people can't jus' find money like this!

J.D. (*Gathering the money*)   Woman, I don't have to argue with you. Here I am with a sack fulla money an' you can't think a nothin' to say to me but that?

SARAH   Now listen, I ain't accusin' you of nothin', all I'm sayin' is . . . you say you found it?

J.D. (*Taking her hands in his*)   Guess what pulled my coat to what was happenin' . . . a dog! An' the funnies' thing about it, I wasn't even plannin' on goin' that way.

SARAH (*Trying to sound positive*)   Well, sometimes we jus' led to do things.

J.D. Yeah, I've heard you say that before, an' today when I finished that wirin' job for ol' lady Saunders she paid me right off, so I decided not to run over to Juke's joint an' take the short cut home.

SARAH I never thought I'd live to see nothin' like this.

J.D. I love to see that expression on your face.

SARAH (*Blushing*) Aw, go on.

J.D. I was jus' walkin' down the street, when all of a sudden . . .

SARAH Wouldn't it be somethin' to move outta this ol' shack after all these years? Yesterday I sold some of my jewelry to a woman livin' on the west side. They got a big pitcher window runnin' cross the whole front. Go on, honey, tell me about it.

J.D. Well all of a sudden this stray lookin' little beat-up dog comes tearin' down the street to beat hell an' almost knocks me over turnin' up the alley.

SARAH This is really somethin'.

J.D. First I figured it was chasin' one a them ol' stray cats in the area, but when I turned up the alley I spied the bag, an' he was sniffin' an' barkin' an' waggin' his behind an carryin' on, baby he was really raisin' cain.

SARAH Who?

J.D. The dog! But the thing struck me weird was the way he looked at me an' started runnin', like he was surprised or scared or somethin'.

SARAH Who?

J.D. The dog, Sarah. Ain't cha listenin'?

SARAH Yeah.

J.D. Sounds funny don't it?

SARAH You can say that again. There's somethin' mighty shady goin' on here.

J.D.   Aw, there's probably a simple explanation for the whole thing. (*Stuffing the empty bag into his pocket*)

SARAH (*Pulling it out, she examines it as though it were contaminated.*)   Tsk, tsk, tsk. These crazy folks got all this money an' leavin' it in the streets . . . My God, J.D., this money belongs to the United States Gov'ment.

J.D.   You jumpin' to conclusions.

SARAH   That's what it says right here on the bag! Fed'ral reserve bank!

J.D. (*Snatching the bag*)   I can read. That don't mean nothin' . . . All in small bills too.

SARAH   Lord have mercy, why didn't chu take it down to the police station?

J.D. (*Stuffing the money into the bag*)   You don't know how to appreciate nothin'. Your Christian upbringin' tellin' you it'd be wrong for me to keep this money Sarah?

SARAH   You know how these folks are about findin' things!

J.D.   Yeah, possession's ninety-nine per cent of the law!

SARAH   Oh honey, I know how you feel. Being' broke jus' changes your whole disposition. I get so discouraged sometimes I jus' sit an' cry, but chu ain't serious about tryin' na keep it, are you?

J.D.   If I ain't, somebody better hurry up an' take me down to the nut house an' lock me in a padded cell.

SARAH   Well, have you thought about how the police are gonna feel about this?

J.D.   Naw! I'm usin' faith!

SARAH   That ain't gonna do you no good, the FBI's gonna be involved in this thing!

J.D.   I knew one day you was gonna admit it. You ain't nothin' but a hypocrite.

SARAH What do you mean by that remark?

J.D. (*Leaving the money on the table*) Ever since we been married you ain't done nothin' but pray to God. You the prayinest woman in the world.

SARAH An' that ain't all, I'm gonna keep *on* prayin'!

J.D. How you know God don't want us to have this money? Maybe this is that reward you been prayin' for. (*Wild laughter off stage*)

SARAH Ain't no sense in you tryin' to put this on God. God ain't got nothin' to do with this an' you know it!

J.D. You know what God's thinkin' too?

SARAH (*Flustered*) Listen . . . Now J.D., Lord, I promised myself I wasn't gonna argue with you today, but mark my word, this ain't nothin' but some trouble.

J.D. Don't chu tell me nothin' about no trouble. There ain't been a day in my life I didn't know trouble, eatin', sleepin', workin', hell jus' tryin' na stay alive. (*Grabbing a fistful of the money*) You see this? This is what they call money, Sarah. Without this everybody's in trouble. This is the only thing in the world anybody gives a damn about. People lie for it, they cheat for it an' beat each other over the heads for it. They're bombin' an' burnin' an' starvin' each other to death for it. These sapsuckers will root like pigs for it. An now they even racin' to the moon for it, an' you want me to turn this money in?

❋   ❋   ❋

Scene from

TO FOLLOW THE PHOENIX

by William Branch

Commissioned by The Delta Sigma Theta Sorority
In Commemoration of the life, work and inspiration of
Mary Church Terrell (1863–1954)

CHARACTERS

ROBERT HEBERTON TERRELL
MARY CHURCH

SCENE

ROBERT HEBERTON TERRELL'S *classroom in the "M" Street
High School in Washington, D.C., 1891. On the blackboard
behind the desk are written several Latin verbs and phrases.*

At rise, ROBERT TERRELL *is seated at his desk, poring over a
pile of examination papers. He is in his early thirties and is
a fine figure of a man. His Harvard background is self-
evident in the cut of his clothes and the preciseness of his
clipped speech.*

TERRELL *sits back for a moment to rest and stretch himself, when he looks off stage. Spying something—or somebody—he quickly turns back to his work and pretends to
busy himself with the conjugations of Latin verbs.*

MARY CHURCH *enters. She is a young woman now, in her
middle twenties, and quite attractive in her "schoolmarm"
outfit. She comes to the desk, but* TERRELL *pretends not to
notice. She steps behind him and looks over his shoulder.*

TERRELL   Cuccurum . . . Cuccuras . . . Cuccurit cursur celeriter ut coronam acciperet.

MARY (*Interrupting*)   You mean: Cuccurit cursur *tam* celeriter, don't you? "He ran so fast *that he might* win the crown." The subjunctive of result rather than the subjunctive of purpose? . . .

TERRELL   Ah, yes. Yes, you're right again, Miss Church. Cuccurit cursur *tam* celeriter. (*He looks up.*) I always said you knew more Latin than I.

MARY (*Smiles*)   Oh, come now, Mr. Terrell. If you don't think I know you deliberately made a slip so as to have an excuse to engage me in conversation, then you must have a very poor estimate of me indeed.

TERRELL   Quite the contrary, Miss Church. My estimate of you is . . . is . . .

MARY   Go on.

TERRELL (*Clearing his throat*)   Won't you sit down . . . ? (*Puts aside his papers and offers her a chair.*) Well, Miss Church, have you finished for the day? No more unruly pupils to be kept after school?

MARY (*Lightly*)   Ha! I'll have you know that none of my students are unruly. They may not all be prize Latin scholars, but at least they have respect.

TERRELL   I'm sure you're right. On both counts.

MARY   But then, of course—being in my class instead of yours, they haven't had the benefit of the latest teaching methods from Harvard.

TERRELL (*Smiles*)   Now, there you go again, Mollie. When are you going to get over the fact that I went to Harvard?

MARY   When are *you* going to get over it?

TERRELL (*Flushes*)   Mollie, that's not being fair.

MARY (*Smiles*) Forgive me, Robert, but it's spring, and I'm feeling sassy as a jaybird this afternoon. You must have patience with me. (*She rises and paces.*) Ah, that I could just stretch forth my arms like wings and fly, fly, fly . . . Oh, to follow the phoenix!

TERRELL Oh . . . ? But why the phoenix? Why not the falcon or the eagle, or even the hawk?

MARY No—never for me any earthbound bird. High as they fly, the phoenix soars still higher. Into the very province of God himself.

TERRELL Hmm . . . Wasn't that the mythical bird of ancient Rome or Greece?

MARY Even earlier, Robert. Back to the early Egyptians. The phoenix was a rare and miraculous bird which appeared only in privileged ages to point the way to righteousness. It was fabled to live for half a thousand years—then to be consumed in flames, only to rise in youthful freshness from its own ashes. (*Looks at him coyly*) Tell me, Robert . . . If I were a phoenix, would you fly away with me?

TERRELL Not unless I were absolutely sure of where you were going.

MARY Oh, Robert. Sometimes I think you have no imagination, no imagination at all.

TERRELL Well, I admit that legal training sometimes leaves a mind somewhat more . . . shall we say, prosaic, than the state you seem to be in today. But I wouldn't go so far as—

MARY (*Interrupts*) That's just it. You wouldn't go so far. Robert, I have known you for all of three years now. And in all that time, you've always made sure you wouldn't go but so far.

TERRELL Now, Mollie. Are you sure you know what you're saying?

MARY Of course. I see no need to beat about the bush. If a

person has something on her mind, I believe in coming right out with it. Say what you mean and mean what you say.

TERRELL (*Uncomfortably*) I'm not sure we should pursue this conversation any further, Miss Church.

MARY Why not? Because I'm a woman and you're a man? Because the woman is supposed to be passive while the man has all the fun of being aggressive?

TERRELL Miss Church . . . !

MARY Well, I think that's just a lot of rot, that's what I think! This whole business of the supposedly reticent female waiting on the male to—to get around to suggesting in the spring what the female's been thinking of all winter long.

TERRELL Mollie, I forbid you to say another word!

MARY You forbid? You see what I mean? Automatically you start ordering me around. Because you're bigger and stronger than I am, I suppose. All right—I grant you that men are physically the more hulking apes. But is that any reason to treat us as if we have any less brains—

TERRELL (*Correcting*) Any fewer brains . . .

MARY —or that women must go on forever playing the same old ridiculous roles you men have assigned us since time immemorial?

TERRELL What in the world did I say to bring on all this?

MARY It's not what you've said, but what you haven't said. What all men haven't said. That women are human beings, too.

TERRELL Oh, I've always granted that.

MARY Equal human beings? With all the very same rights and privileges as men . . . ?

TERRELL Well, now. I'm not sure I'd say exactly that.

MARY And why not? If the principle of equality is to be

accepted at all, mustn't it go the whole way? Can a person be part-way equal? Any more than being part-way pregnant?

TERRELL   Now, see here, Mollie! I don't know what's come over you.

MARY   You men never know. Until it's too late.

TERRELL   Do you feel all right? Can I get you a glass of water? Perhaps a breath of air . . . (*He starts for the window.*)

MARY   Oh, the things we women have to put up with . . . ! If you men only knew what Susan B. Anthony thinks about you.

TERRELL   (*Stops, returns*)   Oh . . . so that's it. Been to another one of those Suffragette meetings, haven't you?

MARY   And what if I have?

TERRELL   Mary, I've told you over and over again—you're wasting your time running around with a bunch of radicals like that. I doubt very much if women in this country will ever get the vote.

MARY   We certainly won't. As long as we have to deal with pig-headed men like you!

TERRELL   Mary, that's insulting! It's uncalled for.

MARY   And I suppose what you've been saying isn't? Oh, but I wish you'd been at the meeting last night. They'd have scratched your eyes out. And I'd a' helped them!

TERRELL   My God! Don't tell me they're counseling violence.

MARY   (*Folding her arms*)   Not yet. But we're considering it.

TERRELL   There's a story in the papers today that a group is marching down Pennsylvania Avenue next week. Why, it's rank insurrection.

MARY   Call it that if you like. I prefer to think we're demonstrating for law and order. A law to acknowledge women's right to vote, and an order to those who oppose us to cease and desist.

TERRELL   Mary, surely you're not planning to join this march.

MARY   Join it? I helped organize it. (TERRELL *turns away, mouthing: "Oh no!"*) We're meeting again tomorrow to plan the details with Miss Anthony herself. We intend to let the world know where we stand. We demand a constitutional amendment that recognizes the right of women to vote and hold public office.

TERRELL   But do you realize what you're doing? Marching in the public streets—why, the police are sure to be out in force. There'll be stringent opposition.

MARY   It won't be the first time.

TERRELL   But what if there's a disturbance? Another riot!

MARY   That would be unfortunate. But we don't intend to attack anyone. And if we're attacked, it only proves our point.

TERRELL   You'd be involved in a public spectacle. You might wind up in jail.

MARY   So we might. And you men would then stand exposed as the tyrannical oppressors you really are.

TERRELL   Never mind about us men. What about you, Mollie? You've got your reputation to think of. Not to mention your job.

MARY   As long as my conscience is clear, I won't worry about my reputation. As for my job, I'd hate very much to lose that.

TERRELL   There, you see—!

MARY   Not because of this pittance of a salary they pay me. But because of the children. And . . . and some of my fellow teachers. I'd miss them terribly.

TERRELL   Then, why risk it, Mollie? Surely you know how much I—er, some of us, would miss you, too.

MARY   (*Turns to him*)   Would you? I mean—would "some of you"?

TERRELL   (*Softly*)   Some of us would, yes. Very much.

MARY (*Giving him her hand*) Oh, Robert . . . (*Then, briskly*) Then all the more reason our march will have been effective. For it will emphasize the human element in our struggle. And if I have to lose my job to prove it, then again, I won't be the first one.

TERRELL (*Angrily*) Mary . . . ! You can't really mean you're willing to risk all these things. All because of a hopeless cause like women's suffrage?

MARY There is nothing hopeless about the cause of women's suffrage! Except the act of opposing it.

TERRELL But surely you know that public sentiment is against the suffragists. Even most of the women are against you.

MARY Since when is right to be determined by mere force of numbers?

TERRELL There is such a thing as majority rule.

MARY Yes—but a majority of all the people. Not just half. Oh, you men make me positively ill! Can't you see it's the same kind of thing we've been fighting in terms of race? If you oppose one double standard, how can you subscribe to another?

TERRELL (*Waves his hand*) All right, all right—don't get yourself any more upset. Sit down. (MARY *glares at him.*) I mean, please. (*She sits, haughtily.*) Now. Mollie, for what it's worth, let me say that I'm inclined—inclined, mind you—to agree with you. Somewhat. Still, there are ways of going about these things. These parades and rallies and marches and being thrown in jail . . . They're just not ladylike.

MARY Of course not! Do you think for one moment that we'd risk ourselves if we could do it any other way?

TERRELL But you, Mollie, I'm concerned about you. You're not cut out for this sort of thing. You are a young lady of great promise. I'd hate to see you ruin your chances for a bright future.

MARY Robert, no future that's worthwhile to me could possibly be ruined because of my active devotion to freedom.

TERRELL (*Frowns*) You're sure of that.

MARY Need you ask?

TERRELL Think, Mary. Are you quite sure?

MARY (*Looks at him, pauses*) Why, yes, Robert. I'm sure.

TERRELL (*Turns away*) I'm sorry you said that, Mary.

MARY But, why?

TERRELL Because it means I've misjudged you. I had thought this business an admirable but harmless passing fancy. But now . . .

MARY (*Rising*) I don't believe I've ever given you cause to think I wasn't serious, Robert. What difference should this make now?

TERRELL We don't have to play games with one another, do we, Mary?

MARY Of course not. I've been trying to convince you of that all along.

TERRELL Well, you've finally succeeded. I'm convinced.

MARY That's not being fair, Robert. You haven't answered my question.

TERRELL What do you want to know?

MARY I want to know what difference this makes now.

TERRELL Can't you guess?

MARY (*Hesitates*) I'd rather not.

TERRELL Mary, you can't expect a man to look upon you as a mature individual, ready for . . . responsibilities, so long as you insist upon playing the rebellious schoolgirl. No matter what your convictions, surely you must see the necessity of being discreet.

MARY Being discreet? About wanting the right to vote? (*Comes to him. Softly.*) Robert . . . Robert Terrell, please answer me truthfully and directly. For this is the most important question I've ever asked anyone in my life. Do you mean to say that there must be a choice between working for my convictions and . . . and having a future with you?

TERRELL   Mary, I . . .

MARY   Tell me, Robert. I have a right to know. Are you asking me to choose?

TERRELL   (*Pauses, paces, then turns*)   No, Mary. I can't do that.

MARY   (*Huskily*)   Thank you, Robert. I don't know what in the world I would have done if you hadn't said that.

TERRELL   Well, I do. You'd 'a flounced out of here with your nose in the air, and it'd take us another two weeks to get back on speaking terms again!

MARY   (*Laughs and comes to him*)   Oh, Robert . . . I'm so lucky to have someone like you. You do understand me, don't you.

TERRELL   Not one blasted bit. But I guess I'd better get used to the idea of having a perennial radical in the family.

MARY   (*Raises her eyebrows*)   Did I hear you correctly, Robert? Are you proposing to me? At long last . . . ?

TERRELL   You're no phoenix—you're a little minx, that's what you are! (*Gestures futilely*) Somehow I have the strangest feeling that my Latin assistant has just taken over the whole department—lock, stock, and barrel.

BLACKOUT

Scene from

"417"

A Drama in one act

by Julian Mayfield

CHARACTERS

GERTRUDE COOLEY, in her early fifties, graying, plump

JAMES LEE COOLEY, a tired young man who looks older than his years

HUBERT COOLEY, husband of Gertrude, father of James Lee. Janitor of building

MISS JONAS, the lady who sells iceys

SCENE

Early evening, 1953; 126th Street in Harlem. We see a suggestion of tenement building and stoop. HUBERT COOLEY *has hit the numbers for five dollars. He has decided to leave his family and start a new life.* MISS JONAS, *near sixty, is sitting at her icey-stand (a little wagon with umbrella over it) near the stoop.* MISS JONAS *knows that the number man has run away because he has no money to pay off on 417.* HUBERT COOLEY *walks out on the stoop, carrying a suitcase.*

MISS JONAS Oh, Mary, don't you weep, don't you moan
Oh, Mary, don't you weep, don't you moan
Pharaoh's army got drownded, Oh, Mary, don't you weep.
One of these mornings bright, and fair
Take my wings and cleave the air,
Pharaoh's army got drownded,
Oh, Mary, don't you weep
(JAMES *walks out to the steps.*)

HUBERT Miss Jonas. Imagine! I have just come through that door for the last time.

MISS JONAS You reckon?

HUBERT I reckon. (HUBERT *crosses over to the left where he sets his valise and sits on top of it.* GERTRUDE *comes on with bag of groceries.*)

GERTRUDE You still here?

HUBERT Don't worry, Gertrude, I'll be out of your way in about ten minutes. What time is it, Miss Jonas?

MISS JONAS (*Taking out pocket watch*) Twenty after five.

HUBERT I'll have to get myself a berth, one of them lowers. A man my age shouldn't sit up all night. They say California's nice this time of year, not too hot, not too cold. I always wanted to take a look at this country the leisurely way. You know, Miss Jonas, the last time I did any traveling was in War One. Just my luck they signed that armistice before I could get overseas.

MISS JONAS Guess those already over didn't object too much.

HUBERT (*Just rambling to nobody in particular*) Well-off white people always traveling. They get on trains and planes and go places just for the hell of it. Only time colored folks travel, they get a telegram somebody's dead and they go down home and bury them. What time is it, Miss Jonas?

MISS JONAS (*Without looking at watch*) A little after five, Mister Hubert.

HUBERT   Got to buy me a watch. Man shouldn't be without a watch. A good one so he can always get to places on time. That's what's wrong with Negroes. They got nothing but cheap watches. John Lewis. He gonna bring the money by and drive me to Grand Central. You ever see that car he rides around in? John Lewis had to pick up the money.

MISS JONAS   Don't guess he gets hit like that every day. Five-dollar hit, near three thousand dollars.

HUBERT   No'm, he sure don't. You can tell that white landlord that Hubert Cooley said he can get himself another slave to be super of these rat traps. Lots of old people go out to California, they say. Sunshine is good for people getting along in age. (*Laughs*) They never thought I'd do it. They laughed at me and said I was crazy as a bedbug. Well, what's that tune the old folks say? You may give a dog a very hard way, but every dog will have its day. (*Laughs*) But I don't hold it against any of the people around here. That's the way it goes. When they meet a man, thinks a little different, acts a little different, they call him nuts. Hell, people thought Jesus Christ was cracked, and look who he turned out to be. Not that there's any comparison, mind you. I was just saying how people are. (HUBERT *continues talking, not to anyone in particular, almost to himself. He is looking down the street for John Lewis.*) And I want you all to know I ain't doing nothing out of spite. I'm just realizing my dreams. You can't fault me for that. What time, Miss Jonas?

MISS JONAS   Nearing six.

HUBERT   Any minute now, John Lewis'll be turning into this block with that long pretty car of his. Come on, John Lewis, come on. Done give this street too much precious time, too much of my life. Give it my youth, give it my strength, almost wasted away around here. Done realized my dream just in time. Ain't gonna give this street no more, no more. Come on John Lewis, come on. (*The lights dim down to black-*

ness. Slowly this is done, for time passes slowly when you are waiting. When they dim back up, no one has moved.)

HUBERT   What time, Miss Jonas, what time?

MISS JONAS   Five after seven, Mister Hubert. (GERTRUDE *goes out to stoop with* JAMES.)

HUBERT   John Lewis hadn't ought to keep a man waiting.

MISS JONAS   You're right. (GERTRUDE *shakes her head to* MISS JONAS.)

MISS JONAS   Unhuh.

JAMES   Tell him to come on in the house, Ma. (GERTRUDE *does not move.*)

JAMES   Ma! . . . I'll do it. (*He goes over to* HUBERT, *who is still waiting for John Lewis to turn into the block.*)

JAMES   (*Quietly*)   Pop, come on inside. It's getting chilly out here. Ma's got dinner almost ready. You must be hungry by now.

HUBERT   Leave me alone, son. I'm waiting for John Lewis.

JAMES   John Lewis is not coming, Pop.

HUBERT   He'll be along. Don't worry.

JAMES   John Lewis had a lot of hits on that number today, Pop, more'n he could pay off. Do you know what that means?

HUBERT   (*Looking at* JAMES *for the first time*)   Means you don't want him to come, that's what it means. (*Laughs, turns away*) I see through you all right, but you'll sing another tune when he gets here.

JAMES   Pop, will you listen to me for a minute, will you?—

HUBERT   Leave me alone—

JAMES   (*Shouting*)   —Are you going to listen to me?—

HUBERT   No. (*Pronouncing*) Jealous, that's what! Nobody wants me to have nothing—

JAMES We want you to have everything that's coming to you, Pop, the money, everything—dammit, you won't listen!—

HUBERT No respect, that's what. No respect for your father. No decent boy would talk to his father that way—

JAMES What other way can I talk to you if you won't listen to what—

HUBERT Boy is jealous of his own father—

JAMES What are we arguing about? I'm only trying to tell you a simple fact. You won't listen to a simple fact.

HUBERT (*Clinging tenaciously to his point*) Jealous, that's what. Pure dee jealous. (JAMES *turns away in a sort of wild frustration. He spreads his hands in anguished despair.*)

JAMES What the hell are you going to do with a guy like this? How do you talk to him? (*Suddenly* JAMES *cannot control himself any more. Blind rage sweeps over him. He turns on* HUBERT.)

HUBERT James Lee! (*In one lunge* JAMES *has snatched his father up from the valise and is holding him in a savage grip.* HUBERT, *the smaller of the two, struggles fiercely but has no chance of escaping, which he soon realizes.*)

JAMES Now you're going to listen to me—

GERTRUDE Don't, James Lee—

JAMES Keep out of this, Ma. For once he's going to look at the world the way it is, not the way he'd like it to be. Today is the day when he is going to learn the facts of life, because I can't afford his ignorance any more, because I'm young and there're a few things I'd like to do with my life rather than play wet nurse to a fifty-one-year-old man. Because my mother is not young any more. She's tired and she's had too many rough breaks, and she can't afford to play wet nurse to that fifty-one-year-old man. (GERTRUDE *is stopped.* JAMES *turns away from her to his father.*) Now, Pop, this is a street. That's what it is, a street. (*Stamps foot on pavement*)

You can see it, you can feel it, you can hear it, and you can smell it. (*Kicks trashcan*) That's what is known as a trashcan. When you've got something you absolutely can't use any more, you put it in the trashcan. See, trashcan. See it, feel it (*Kicks it again*) hear it and smell it. (*Nods head toward tenement house*) Believe it or not, they call that a house, see, feel, smell. (*Indicates self*) Man. (*Indicates* GERTRUDE) Woman. Real things. Touch, see, hear, smell. These are things which exist. Now let's talk about John Lewis and your three thousand dollars. I told you that John Lewis had so many hits on that number that he couldn't pay off. So he got in his car and left town. But you say he's coming down the street. Well, Pop, show him to me. Let me see him. Touch him. Let's see the green of that loot. Or is this just another one of those dreams?

HUBERT (*Beginning to stir*) James Lee!

JAMES Are you going to spend the rest of your life waiting for John Lewis to bring you your treasure chest or are you going to wake up and live? Answer me! (*Shakes* HUBERT.)

GERTRUDE James Lee, let him go.

JAMES He's got to see this, Ma. None of us can go on like we've been. (*To* HUBERT) You see, Pop, it's very important to me because there's a girl named Essie that I'd like to marry, but I hardly ever get a chance to see her. Ma and I are too busy looking after you. I called her up a little while back but she said she might be busy tonight. Then I remembered that last night we were supposed to do a simple thing like go to the movie. But I was looking for my father. Imagine! I was so busy trying to find you that I forgot all about my girl. So you see I want to know what you intend to do, Pop, because I'm going to get married. Huh, Pop?

GERTRUDE I don't want to see this! Let him go! Let him go! (*She begins to strike* JAMES *with her fists. He releases* HUBERT, *turns away, bewildered, anguished.* JAMES *sits down on a corner of the steps.* MISS JONAS *has backed away.* HUBERT *sits back on the valise, puzzled, shocked, straining his eyes to see what is really down the street, torn by the truth of what* JAMES LEE *has said.* GERTRUDE *stands over her son.*)

GERTRUDE   So maybe you're strong and Hubert Cooley's not so strong. Maybe you think you know a few things about facing up to life and he don't—

JAMES (*Trembling*)   I'm sorry, Ma—

GERTRUDE   The first nine years we were married, Hubert Cooley tried to make a go of seven little businesses—

JAMES   I'm sorry, Ma—

GERTRUDE   Shut your mouth and listen! Seven businesses. A candy store, a record shop, and everything else you don't need during a depression. And he never made a dime, not one thin dime out of one of them. But he'd go back and he'd work and save and try something else. But what do you do when there's nothing else left to try? That's when he started with this numbers thing, playing them like his life depended on them. So maybe he's a fool. God knows, I think so sometimes. But he tried. That makes him somebody. You get that? Somebody! (*Exhausted*) I don't know what to do. Can't even be mad at him no more. 'S like kicking him when he's down.

JAMES   Ma, we can't let him hold onto that stupid dream of his. It's rough out here and he's got to face it like everybody else. Dreams won't get it.

GERTRUDE   I don't know if that's so exactly. You run into some rough spots passing through here and sometimes they're hard to get over. That's when a dream comes in handy. (*She goes down to* HUBERT *who still sits on the valise. He is not looking down the street any more. His head is bowed.*) Hubert.

HUBERT (*Avoiding her eyes*)   Don't laugh at me, Gertrude. I wouldn't laugh at you.

GERTRUDE   Who's laughing, man?

HUBERT   Never meant to hurt you, Gertrude—

GERTRUDE   I know you didn't—

HUBERT Just don't like it around here, that's all.

GERTRUDE We live where we can and we do what we can. (HUBERT *looks up at* MRS. COOLEY *for the first time. A smile crosses his face.*)

HUBERT Doggone, Gertrude, if I ain't the hardest-luck man in the whole wide world. Don't nothing ever come right for me. Remember that time I hustled up on that thousand dollars and rented that store on 140th Street?

GERTRUDE (*Laughing*) Oh, Lord.

HUBERT And two days later the banks closed down. I should've took my cue then. (*He stops laughing, and a disturbing thought crosses him.*) You know, Gertrude, it's not good around here. Babies are born here and old folks die here, and in between you can't even do a little bit of living.

GERTRUDE Oh, we'll live. That's the only thing I'm ever sure of. (JAMES *comes over to them. Now he is the son again.*)

JAMES I'll take your bag in, Pop.

HUBERT I'll take it in. I brought it out, didn't I?

JAMES Yessir.

HUBERT And you want to control yourself when you're making a point. Stop pulling on my rags. Don't get so excited. Good night, Miss Jonas. Wonder what I ought to try next. There's got to be some way to win.

JAMES Sure, Pop, there's got to be. (*They go into the house. The lights dim down.* MISS JONAS *has packed her equipment. Another day is done. She pushes her cart off stage.*)

＊　　＊　　＊

Scene from
THE DAUBERS
by Theodore Ward

CHARACTERS

 MYRA ZETON COLE, an elderly Negro woman
 BYRLE, her granddaughter
 INEZ, her daughter-in-law
 CLEMENTINE, their maid

TIME   Spring 1950

SCENE

 *The living room-dining room of the Coles in Forrestville
 Avenue, Chicago. A large spacious room with a balcony and
 stairway on the right, and a broad arch separating the living
 from the dining room up left. As middle-class as possible.*
 MRS. COLE *is working in water color at a small easel near
 the bay window, ostensibly reproducing a scene of Washington Park, which can evidently be seen in the curve of the
 window. She is a Negro woman of sixty-five, quite refined.
 Her hair is slightly gray, and her broad, copper-colored
 features give her the aspect of an American Indian.* BYRLE
 enters from her room.

COLE (*Seeing* BYRLE *in riding habit*) Where're you going in that outfit?

BYRLE Teresa and I have a date. We're going to canter over to the lake and back before dinner.

COLE Well, call her and break it.

BYRLE But, Grandma, darling! I can't do that. What'll Teresa think?

COLE That's immaterial to me. I want to see you do your homework.

BYRLE What old homework?

COLE (*Warningly*) I don't want to have to speak to Inez.

BYRLE It makes no difference to me whether you speak to Mother or not. I have no homework.

COLE How do you ever expect to graduate?

BYRLE What makes you think I won't?

COLE The report I've had.

BYRLE Has the principal been writing to you?

COLE No. But you don't seem to realize, Byrle; you're being watched all the time.

BYRLE So what?

COLE I've tried to tell you; any failure on your part will be interpreted only too readily as proof of Negro inferiority.

BYRLE I don't know whom you've been discussing me with. But for your information, nothing a Negro student does is ever appreciated at Jackson High.

COLE Haven't I told you before: no Negro can expect recognition of his work, or support either for that matter, from white people?

BYRLE That's exactly why I don't see why you should worry!

COLE You're allowing prejudice to discourage you, when the big thing is to go straight ahead, and never swerve from your own sense of duty!

BYRLE You're all right, Grandma dear. But you're so wrong it's pitiful.

COLE I wasn't born yesterday. I know how easy it is for you or any other Negro child to get the idea; in the eyes of the world you don't count.

BYRLE Do I, Grandma? Tell me, *really?*

COLE You're human, regardless of how others may see you. But you've got to ask yourself, am I going to allow myself to be defeated just because of the color of my skin, or is there something I can do about making a success of my life? You have got to stop and take stock. You've got to ask yourself, what are my assets?

BYRLE Suppose you tell me.

COLE Well, for one thing: you're seventeen. You're attractive. You've a good brain and every advantage to prove yourself fit and make a real contribution to the race—

BYRLE And what else, Grandma?

COLE I'm going to leave you this house. Between Inez and your father, you'll have money. What more could a person need to succeed in life?

BYRLE (*Touched*) You're sweet, Grandma—as sweet as you can be. And I appreciate your wanting to leave me the house. But you don't have to promise me anything like that. I'd make you proud of me if I could. But I can't change myself. I guess it's just that nothing around here appeals to me . . . and that goes for all this talk about the race. I don't even care about prejudice. I'm an American and I guess I want to be treated like one. But if it can't be like that, then I say the devil with it!

COLE You can't fight prejudice, Byrle, by pretending you don't care!

BYRLE (*Easily*) I'm not pretending, dear. I'm detached.

COLE "Detached," are you? I imagine a turtle thinks the same way when he pulls in his neck. But it doesn't stop the fisherman from carrying him on to market! No, my dear, you can only defeat prejudice by attacking it at its very roots.

BYRLE How do you mean?

COLE By developing the highest moral standards and proving your right to be respected and treated as an equal.

BYRLE You're too deep for me.

COLE I mean by studying the past. What they say about the Negro today, for example, might just as easily have been said about the ancient Romans, when they were nothing but barbarians alongside of the Babylonians. Yet, the Romans were destined to build a culture which still affects civilization. You've got to learn from the Jews. You can't tell one from any other kind of white person. Yet, they're belittled and discriminated against, though they hold as high a place as any in the fields of science, industry, and art.

BYRLE Now you're contradicting yourself.

COLE I cite the Jews because they're "happy idealists"! They know how to go on and conquer regardless.

BYRLE What can a Negro do besides open an undertaking parlor or sell beer!

COLE You haven't seen the changes I have, child. Otherwise, you'd know our opportunity beckons as never before.

BYRLE Oh yeah? What about Ann Burns? What about Tony Chilton?

COLE (*Barking*) Who are they?—One, an artist who never paints! The other, a composer who hasn't completed a single major work! Don't mention such "crepe-hangers" to me! You can find them a dime a dozen on any corner, shedding tears about prejudice and the lack of opportunity instead of buckling down and doing some work.

BYRLE   I'll study when I come back. I've got to meet Teresa.

COLE   I told you you weren't going out of here!

BYRLE   (*Stubbornly*)   I'm not going to keep the date. I just want to see her for a minute.

COLE   I'm sorry. But I say no!

BYRLE   (*Sharply*)   But I'll be right back, I tell you. I've got to see her!

INEZ   (*Entering in time to hear the last remark—a smartly dressed woman of forty in a chic suit and mink scarf*)   What is it now?

BYRLE   (*Flaring automatically with deep-seated resentment*)   Oh, you! You always have to butt in!

INEZ   (*Hurt and indignant*)   Don't you talk to me like that!

BYRLE   (*Stubbornly*)   I'm talking to Grandma.

INEZ   (*Angrily*)   I don't care!—And just for that, whatever it is, you're not going to do it!

BYRLE   I don't care either!

CLEM   (*Entering from kitchen*)   Hello, Inez. You goin' to be home for dinner?

INEZ   (*Gruffly*)   No! Don't bother me! (*Going to desk, she begins searching for some article*)   I'm due at my place on Drexel. I've got to meet the damn plumber and let *him* rob me—but you might leave me a snack I can warm later.

BYRLE   Clementine, what's for dessert?

CLEM   (*Smiling*)   Apple cobbler!

BYRLE   Oh, goody. I'll take some and a cup of tea maybe.

INEZ   (*Still searching*)   This is no cafeteria! You'll wait and sit down and eat properly.

BYRLE   But I don't want dinner.

CLEM   How you can expect, child, to keep your health, beats me!

BYRLE (*Petulantly*) All of a sudden, everybody's anxious about me!

CLEM But, Honey, you can't live off of sweets—

BYRLE (*Sharply*) Never mind! You're not the doctor!

CLEM (*Hurt—going*) Excuse me—

BYRLE (*Running to catch her, contritely*) I really didn't mean that, Clem.

CLEM (*Patting her hand*) I know you didn't, honey. (*Exit to kitchen.*)

BYRLE (*Saunters down to watch her mother for a moment—then*) Mother, did you get the tickets for Sunday?

INEZ (*Preoccupiedly*) What tickets—?

BYRLE (*Annoyed*) I knew it!

INEZ (*Turning*) What tickets are you talking about?

BYRLE Marion Anderson's concert—and it's her last appearance.

INEZ (*Going on with her search*) Oh, that—well. I simply won't be able to manage it. Your daddy wants me to drive out to Floral Park Sunday to look at a house he wants to buy!

BYRLE But you promised to take me!

INEZ (*Halting. Annoyed*) Look, Byrle. You're a big girl now. Sunday afternoon's the only time the people will be home out there. I'll give you the money for the tickets, and perhaps you and Mama can go.

BYRLE You never do anything I want.

INEZ (*Searching again*) Don't exaggerate!

BYRLE You know very well everybody who's anybody is going to be there Sunday.

INEZ So will you.

BYRLE (*Bitterly*) Yeah! Trailing behind Grandma, like something the cat dragged in!

COLE Well!

BYRLE I meant no offense, Grandma. But Mother and I are never seen anywhere together any more!

INEZ (*Ironically*) I didn't know you took such pride in me, darling. I'm flattered. But I can't play the fool and neglect the business.

BYRLE I'm not important.

INEZ (*Coldly*) Why are you trying to pick a quarrel with me?

BYRLE (*Shocked*) Well, I like that!

INEZ You act like it. You've nothing to complain of. You belong to one of Chicago's first families. You've inherited your grandfather's good name, and Daddy and I are going to see to it you have every material advantage—that is, if you let us. However, I'm not going to waste valuable time coddling you! (*Turning, she starts into her room.*)

BYRLE (*Bitterly*) You don't care!

INEZ (*Whirling at door*) Can't you understand? Between my desk in the City Hall and your father's property, I've enough to drive me into a nervous breakdown! You know your daddy has no time to look after the business!

BYRLE What good is my position in society if I never go into it?

INEZ I can't be bothered with the doings of society! Look to me to prepare the way for you. But beyond that, let me alone! (*She starts within again.*)

BYRLE All I get from you is neglect!

INEZ (*Crossing to shake her*) You spineless, ungrateful worm!

BYRLE Let go of me!

INEZ When have you been deprived of anything? Right this minute you're wearing an outfit that cost me a hundred and fifty dollars—a habit you won't find on any girl this side of the Gold Coast!

BYRLE (*Driven by unconscious necessity*) You don't love me!

INEZ (*Distressed*) What more am I to do—spend the rest of my life pampering you to disprove that?

BYRLE (*Hysterically*) You can't disprove it! You can't. You know it's true! You don't care for me. All you care about is those damn flats and kitchenettes. I hate you!

INEZ (*Furious, with a sense of frustration*) Just for that, get upstairs to your room! And you'll not go to the concert either!

BYRLE (*Running up*) I don't give a damn! (*Exit above.*)

INEZ (*Beaten*) Oh, I could kill her!

COLE (*Quietly*) The child's struggling for her rights.

INEZ (*Distrustfully*) Are you trying to take up for her?

COLE You know better.

INEZ I can't stand her impudence. She's become unbearable!

COLE Still, you can't afford to lose her trust.

INEZ (*In growing despair*) She doesn't like me. Like she says, she hates me. All she wants is to hurt me. And why? What've I done to deserve it? Everytime I try to come close to her, she's ready to stick a knife in my heart! (*Turning, she goes within.*)

COLE (*Following her to door*) It's hard, Inez. Anyway you look at it. Nevertheless, she's right about your not spending enough time with her.

INEZ (*Bouncing out*) Are you trying to criticize my efforts to make a success of the business?

COLE No. I'd be the last to oppose what you're trying to do. Our progress as a people depends upon our getting into and making a success of all lines. (INEZ, *satisfied, goes in again.*) But I've been over the road you're traveling. I think you're making the mistake I made with Bob. I put too much faith in my *own capacity*, and not enough in *love* and *trust* in him to find his own way—what was good for him, rather than what I thought was the safest attitude toward life.

INEZ   I'm going to pack her off to Fisk next fall, and get her out of my sight!

BYRLE   (*Ambiguously, as she appears again*)   Fisk—?

INEZ   Yes, Fisk! Any objections?

BYRLE   (*Coldly*)   Yes. I think you might've consulted me!

INEZ   Never mind! You need at least two years at Fisk.

COLE   (*Agreeing*)   Or Howard or Atlanta!

BYRLE   (*Sarcastically*)   Ha! What about Vassar? What about Barnard?

INEZ   I'm thinking of your future.

BYRLE   What old future?

COLE   (*Sympathetically*)   You must have the necessary background, child. Your position in society is going to demand it tomorrow.

BYRLE   Ha! Ha! As if there weren't enough Spooks in my background.

INEZ   Don't act like an unadulterated ass! It's a matter of pride in your own people and their traditions!

BYRLE   That's a laugh! And I'm not for it!

INEZ   (*Firmly*)   Whether you are or not, you'll go. And I don't want to hear any more about it.

BYRLE   You forget I'm not a child any more!

INEZ   You're still a minor; and you'll do as you're told, or I'll put you away! Do you understand that? I'll send you to reform school! You fool with me! Just try it and see!

COLE   (*Noticing her searching again*)   What do you keep looking for. Inez?

INEZ   (*She remains silent for a moment, then feigns casualness*)   It's my billfold—Neither of you have seen it, have you?

COLE   No. Not I.

BYRLE (*Sauntering off*)   Nor I, either.

INEZ (*Watching* BYRLE—*and calling*)   Clementine?—I know I had it when I came home last night.

COLE   When did you miss it?

INEZ   This morning, when I stopped for gas (*Seeing* CLEMENTINE *enter*) Did you see my billfold when you were cleaning my room this morning?

CLEM   No. Did you lose it?

INEZ   Yes, though I can't see how. The house wasn't burglarized. (*To* CLEM) But it's all right. You may go.

CLEM (*Going*)   I'll take pains and look round for it, soon's I get out of the kitchen.

INEZ   You needn't bother. I've been through everything with a fine-toothed comb. (*Exit* CLEM.)

COLE   Did you lose anything of value?

INEZ   A hundred and thirty-five dollars, or about that.

COLE   Good Lord!

INEZ (*Watching* BYRLE, *who has picked up a magazine*)   I collected the rent from the Sterlings—that was eighty dollars, and I must've had around fifty dollars when I left the City Hall.

COLE   What about Bob—did you ask him?

INEZ   Bob never touches a dime without telling me—in fact, he never fails to give me a check for anything he takes, so I can keep my accounts straight—Byrle, are you *sure* you didn't see it?

BYRLE (*Hurling magazine away*)   What do you mean, am I sure? I told you, didn't I?

INEZ (*Doubtfully*)   Well, you needn't fly off the handle!

BYRLE (*Indignantly*)   I told you once. Yet you ask me again, as if I'm a liar. As if I'm a thief! I don't know anything about your damn billfold. But you've got to single me out. Am I the only one who lives in this house?

INEZ   You heard me ask others.

BYRLE   But you let it go at that. Why pick on me? As if you were trying to accuse me? For all you know, you might've laid your damn bag down someplace and some thief went through it!

COLE   That seems likely.

INEZ   I'm certain I had it in my bag when I went to bed.

BYRLE (*Angrily*)   In other words, I took it!

INEZ (*Coldly*)   The way you've been acting lately, I wouldn't put it past you!

BYRLE (*Outraged*)   Do you hear that, Grandma!

COLE   Inez, I've never known her to be dishonest.

INEZ   There's a first time to everything!

BYRLE   You're a liar!

INEZ   Don't you call me a liar!

BYRLE   You are a liar, if you say I took it!

INEZ (*Defensively*)   I didn't say you took it. I said I don't trust you any more.

BYRLE   And why? Because you haven't got the nerve to accuse me directly. But I'll get even with you. You'll see if I don't!

INEZ   I don't care anything about your threats! And if you think you're getting away with anything, you'll find out different. I'm going to check up on you. If you took that money, there was absolutely no cause for it. Nobody ever refuses you anything. Your daddy gives you ten dollars a week—to say nothing of what you get from your aunt Toy and Mama there, and me on the side. You don't need clothes. Your closet is bursting with things you never wear, and you know my account is open to you at both Mandel's and Field's! (*Going*) But I'll find out! And if I do, I'll show you a trick or two!

BYRLE You go to hell!

INEZ (*Striding back*) I do what? (*Slapping her*) Maybe that'll close your dirty mouth!

BYRLE (*Running above*) You stinker! Oh, I'll get you for this! (*Halting on balcony*) You'll see if I don't.

*   *   *

Scene from
ONE LAST LOOK
by Steve Carter

CHARACTERS

ORGANIST	FUNERAL DIRECTOR
SOPRANO	REVA
EUSTACE BAYLOR	DONNA
CORA LEE SIMMONS	APRIL BAYLOR
ADELAIDE	

A FEW FRIENDS AND OTHER RELATIVES

TIME   Now

SCENE
   There is complete blackness.

CORA LEE Yeah . . . this is the place. I remember from when we buried my youngest sister's old man. This is the same place.

ADELAIDE I been to some funerals here too. Can't remember whose . . . but this place looks familiar. You goin' to the wake later on?

CORA LEE Hungry as I am . . . I wouldn't miss it. You know, I couldn't stop and get nothin' to eat . . . had to come here straight from work . . . Reva always did make good potato salad . . . sure hope she made some for tonight. (*In the darkness an organ starts to play almost inaudibly. Slowly the lights come up. The* SOPRANO *is buxom, bewigged and understated passion. She is downstage center. To her left is a lectern, behind her is a casket. The casket is open, we cannot see the occupant; it is flower-laden. The lights go higher and we see the figure of* EUSTACE BAYLOR *a little behind the casket.* SOPRANO *sings "Abide with Me" as* EUSTACE *looks down on his "mortal remains." There is a center aisle. There is a seat for the* SOPRANO *when she is not singing.* CORA LEE *and* ADELAIDE *find seats behind the family rows. LIGHTS UP.*)

ADELAIDE (*To the old bunch*) How do . . . ? Hi, sweetheart. I never knew he had so many friends.

CORA LEE He didn't. It's just a whole lot of people can't believe he's dead . . . so they come to make sure he ain' foolin'.

ADELAIDE Ain't you gonna look in the casket?

CORA LEE What for? He's in there, ain't he?

ADELAIDE Come on, gal. Don't be 'fraid . . . Dead people can't hurt you none . . . Let's look in . . . (*She goes up to casket*) I guess he caused a whole lot of women to laugh.

CORA LEE . . . and cry.

FUNERAL DIRECTOR (*Enters with studied solemnity*) All rise. Everyone please rise. (REVA *and her children enter.*)

ADELAIDE   Look at Reva's dress. Lord, don't make me laugh out loud. Never did know how to dress. That's probably why he never took her out nowhere. (*As* REVA *and children pass*) Reva, darlin', I'm so sorry. My sympathy.

REVA   Thank you.

CORA LEE   Don't you lose heart, now.

ADELAIDE   You done your job, now God gonna do his.

REVA   Thank you so much. (FUNERAL DIRECTOR *offers them his sympathy.* REVA *and family sit.*)

ADELAIDE   Poor thing. She fightin' that dress, ain't she?

FUNERAL DIRECTOR (*As they all sit*)   We gather to pay our last respects to our departed brother, Eustace Baylor. His favorite hymn.

SOPRANO (*Stands over Butler family and sings*)   "Nearer My God to Thee" . . . etc.

CORA LEE   He never knew what the inside of a church looked like, much less had a favorite hymn . . . Remember his old saying, "What I don't do today, I ain't gonna do tomorrow."

ADELAIDE   Look at his son. That boy's head's so nappy you could get lost in it.

CORA LEE   One of them Hundred Twenty-fifth Street Africans.

ADELAIDE   He ain't nothing 'cept dirty. His shirt's dirty . . . His shoes' dirty . . . He's dirty . . . He sure didn't take after his father. Eustace always was clean . . . even if he was a dirty dog. The gal ain't much better . . . She like her momma . . . They look frowsy. (*More people enter.*)

CORA LEE   I wouldn't have missed this for the world . . . Lord! Lord! Lord!

FUNERAL DIRECTOR   Friends, I have been asked to be brief because Eustace Baylor's stay on this earth was brief. Eustace was almost sixty but he had lived so much . . . so fast . . . and probably never lived at all . . . but he had so much life left that it seemed, to those who knew and possibly loved him . . . that he was here all too briefly. (*He and others freeze in their places.* DONNA *rises during the "freeze of motion" and addresses her father who is sitting by his casket.*)

DONNA (*Approaching casket*) Daddy, why am I thirty-four years old . . . with nine kids . . . and looking like I was fifty? . . . Can you tell me anything?

EUSTACE Missy, I can't give you the answers now . . . but don't hate me. I did my best for you and . . . I loved you.

DONNA But you kept me down. Every man I ever met was you, Daddy, you all over again. I loved you so much that I had to love them . . . Guess it's my lot to go through life falling for no-good men . . . or men who ain't good for me.

EUSTACE I still don't know if there's a God, but if there is, I sure wish He'd let me feel . . . again . . .

DONNA I feel enough for both of us, Daddy . . . Good-by. I loved you so. (*Sits.*)

FUNERAL DIRECTOR (*As all come out of "freeze"*) Eustace and I were children together in Richmond. We were friends. We went to school together and we came north to this city together. (*Pleased with himself*) We all knew Eustace, knew him as a man with faults . . . but he was honest. (*All freeze except* APRIL . . . *who rises.*)

APRIL You were honest. Remember how honest you were when I was fifteen? Told me I should marry somebody . . . anybody . . . so you wouldn't have to support me any more? . . .

EUSTACE I had two good reasons.

APRIL You certainly did. One was a fifth . . . the other a quart.

EUSTACE You never did understand me.

APRIL I needed you . . . to tell me I was Daddy's girl.

EUSTACE You had your mother.

APRIL She was too busy being a father to be a mother . . . too busy doing your job . . . to do hers.

EUSTACE She should have realized you needed a father.

APRIL Don't you criticize my mother. She tried to get someone to be a father to us but we wouldn't accept it. We wanted our own father.

EUSTACE I sent you toys at Christmas and you never even thanked me . . . I couldn't stand just being tolerated.

APRIL I loathed the toys because I loathed Christmas. Christmas was a time for daddies. Where were you?

EUSTACE It's too late to be sorry.

APRIL It is too late . . . too late for me even to forgive you. (*Sits.*)

EUSTACE Oh, God. Let me have some feeling. I have to feel something. Is the soul dead too? They always said the soul never died . . . That the soul was the feeling place. Why can't I feel?

FUNERAL DIRECTOR Whatever his faults, and he may have had many, we have to forgive him now . . . because we are only mortal. (REVA *rises as others freeze.*)

REVA You goin' to your grave not knowin' me. Thinkin' that I was so crazy in love with you that that was the reason I put up with all the hurtin' you put on me. I never loved you. I only *needed* you. Before you . . . there was nobody . . . there was only my folks telling me I was big, dumb, clumsy, stupid . . . ugly.

EUSTACE You hold yourself lightly.

REVA They held me . . . you and them . . . held me lightly. Me . . . with all that lovely feelin' inside of me . . . and nobody willin' to take it. Me . . . who wanted to read books and go to plays and talk about things goin' on in the world. But all that is over with. I'm gettin' old. There's new things and new kinds of people . . . I ain't gonna fit in. (*Weeps aloud*) And I got to face it by myself . . . all by myself! (*Collapsing in her seat, she screams back to reality.*)

FUNERAL DIRECTOR To conclude. I should like to ask the Lord on behalf of my sleeping friend . . . to protect his soul and forgive him his sins. Let us pray.

SOPRANO (*Sings*) Oh, when I come to the end of my journey . . . etc.

EUSTACE I walked through this life and didn't prove a thing. (*Shakes his head with a sardonic smile* . . . SOPRANO *continues* . . . *family and friends softly weep.*)

❋   ❋   ❋

Lorraine Hansberry wrote her mother a letter about *A Raisin in the Sun.*

January 19, 1959   Hotel Taft, New Haven, Connecticut

Dear Mother,
Well—here we are. I am sitting alone in a nice hotel room in New Haven, Connecticut. Downstairs, next door, in the Shubert Theatre, technicians are putting the finishing touches on a living room that is supposed to be a Chicago living room. Wednesday the curtain goes up at 8 P.M. The next day the New Haven papers will say what they think about our efforts. A great deal of money has been spent and a lot of people have done some hard, hard work. And it may be the beginning of many different careers.

The actors are very good and the director is a very talented man—so if it is a poor show I won't be able to blame a soul but your youngest daughter.

Mama, it is a play that tells the truth about people, Negroes and life and I think it will help a lot of people to understand how we are just as complicated as they are—and just as mixed up—but above all, that we have among our miserable and downtrodden ranks—people who are the very essence of human dignity. That is what, after all the laughter and tears, the play is supposed to say. I hope it will make you very proud. Love to all,

Scene from

A RAISIN IN THE SUN

by Lorraine Hansberry

CHARACTERS

MAMA	BENEATHA
RUTH	LINDNER
WALTER	TRAVIS

SCENE

MAMA *enters from her bedroom. She is lost, vague, trying to catch hold, to make some sense of her former command of the world, but it still eludes her. A sense of waste overwhelms her gait; a measure of apology rides on her shoulders. She goes to her plant, which has remained on the table, looks at it, picks it up and takes it to the window sill and sits it outside, and she stands and looks at it a long moment. Then she closes the window, straightens her body with effort, and turns around to her children.*

MAMA Well—ain't it a mess in here, though? (*A false cheerfulness, a beginning of something*) I guess we all better stop moping around and get some work done. All this unpacking and everything we got to do. (RUTH *raises her head slowly in response to the sense of the line; and* BENEATHA *in similar manner turns very slowly to look at her mother.*) One of you all better call the moving people and tell 'em not to come.

RUTH Tell 'em not to come?

MAMA Of course, baby. Ain't no need in 'em coming all the way here and having to go back. They charges for that too. (*She sits down, fingers to her brow, thinking.*) Lord, ever since I was a little girl, I always remembers people saying, "Lena—Lena Eggleston, you aims too high all the time. You needs to slow down and see life a little more like it is. Just slow down some." That's what they always used to say down home—"Lord, that Lena Eggleston is a high-minded thing. She'll get her due one day!"

RUTH No, Lena . . .

MAMA Me and Big Walter just didn't never learn right.

RUTH Lena, no! We gotta go, Bennie—tell her. (*She rises and crosses to* BENEATHA *with her arms outstretched.* BENEATHA *doesn't respond.*) Tell her we can still move . . . the notes ain't but a hundred and twenty-five a month. We got four grown people in this house—we can work . . .

MAMA (*To herself*) Just aimed too high all the time—

RUTH (*Turning and going to* MAMA *fast—the words pouring out with urgency and desperation*) Lena—I'll work . . . I'll work twenty hours a day in all the kitchens in Chicago . . . I'll strap my baby on my back if I have to and scrub all the floors in America and wash all the sheets in America if I have to—but we got to move . . . We got to get out of here. (MAMA *reaches out absently and pats* RUTH's *hand.*)

MAMA No—I sees things differently now. Been thinking 'bout some of the things we could do to fix this place up some. I seen a secondhand bureau over on Maxwell Street just the other day that could fit right there. (*She points to where the new furniture might go.* RUTH *wanders away from her.*) Would need some new handles on it and then a little varnish and then it look like something brand-new. And—we can put up them new curtains in the kitchen . . . Why this place be looking fine. Cheer us all up so that we forget trouble ever came. (*To* RUTH) And you could get some nice screens to put up in your room round the baby's bassinet. (*She looks at both of them pleadingly.*) Sometimes you just got to know when to give up some things . . . and hold on to what you got. (WALTER *enters from the outside, looking spent and leaning against the door, his coat hanging from him*)

MAMA Where you been, son?

WALTER (*Breathing hard*) Made a call.

MAMA To who, son?

WALTER To The Man.

MAMA What man, baby?

WALTER The Man, Mama. Don't you know who The Man is?

RUTH Walter Lee?

WALTER *The Man.* Like the guys in the streets say—The Man. Captain Boss—Mistuh Charley—Old Captain Please Mr. Bossman . . .

BENEATHA (*Suddenly*) Lindner!

WALTER That's right! That's good. I told him to come right over.

BENEATHA (*Fiercely, understanding*) For what? What do you want to see him for!

WALTER (*Looking at his sister*) We going to do business with him.

MAMA What you talking 'bout, son?

WALTER Talking 'bout life, Mama. You all always telling me to see life like it is. Well—I laid in there on my back today . . . and I figured it out. Life just like it is. Who gets and who don't get. (*He sits down with his coat on and laughs.*) Mama, you know it's all divided up. Life is. Sure enough. Between the takers and the "tooken." (*He laughs.*) I've figured it out finally. (*He looks around at them.*) Yeah. Some of us always getting "tooken." (*He laughs.*) People like Willy Harris, they don't never get "tooken." And you know why the rest of us do? 'Cause we all mixed up. Mixed up bad. We get to looking 'round for the right and the wrong; and we worry about it and cry about it and stay up nights trying to figure out 'bout the wrong and the right of things all the time . . . And all the time, man, them takers is out there operating, just taking and taking. Willy Harris? Shoot—Willy Harris don't even count. He don't even count in the big scheme of things. But I'll say one thing for old Willy Harris . . . he's taught me something. He's taught me to keep my eye on what counts in this world. Yeah. (*Shouting out a little*) Thanks, Willy!

RUTH What did you call that man for, Walter Lee?

WALTER Called him to tell him to come on over to the show. Gonna put on a show for the man. Just what he wants to see. You see, Mama, the man came here today and he told us that them people out there where you want us to move— well they so upset they willing to pay us not to move out there. (*He laughs again.*) And—and, oh, Mama—you would of been proud of the way me and Ruth and Bennie acted. We told the man to get out. Oh, we was some proud folks this afternoon, yeah. (*He lights a cigarette.*) We were still full of that old-time stuff . . .

RUTH (*Coming toward him slowly*) You talking 'bout taking them people's money to keep us from moving in that house?

WALTER I ain't just talking 'bout it, baby—I'm telling you that's what's going to happen.

BENEATHA   Oh, God! Where is the bottom! Where is the real honest-to-God bottom so he can't go any farther!

WALTER   See—that's the old stuff. You and that boy that was here today. You all want everybody to carry a flag and a spear and sing some marching songs, huh? You wanna spend your life looking into things and trying to find the right and the wrong part, huh? Yeah. You know what's going to happen to that boy someday—he'll find himself sitting in a dungeon, locked in forever—and the takers will have the key! Forget it, baby! There ain't no causes—there ain't nothing but taking in this world, and he who takes most is smartest—and it don't make a damn bit of difference *how*.

MAMA   You making something inside me cry, son. Some awful pain inside me.

WALTER   Don't cry, Mama. Understand. That white man is going to walk in that door able to write checks for more money than we ever had. It's important to him and I'm going to help him . . . I'm going to put on the show, Mama.

MAMA   Son—I come from five generations of people who was slaves and sharecroppers—but ain't nobody in my family never let nobody pay 'em no money that was a way of telling us we wasn't fit to walk the earth. We ain't never been that poor. (*Raising her eyes and looking at him*) We ain't never been that dead inside.

BENEATHA   Well—we are dead now. All the talk about dreams and sunlight that goes on in this house. All dead.

WALTER   What's the matter with you all! I didn't make this world! It was give to me this way! Hell, yes, I want me some yachts someday! Yes, I want to hang some real pearls 'round my wife's neck. Ain't she supposed to wear no pearls? Somebody tell me—tell me, who decides which women is suppose to wear pearls in this world. I tell you I am a *man* —and I think my wife should wear some pearls in this world! (*This last line hangs a good while and* WALTER *begins to move about the room. The word "Man" has penetrated his consciousness; he mumbles it to himself repeatedly between strange agitated pauses as he moves about.*)

MAMA   Baby, how you going to feel on the inside?

WALTER   Fine! . . . Going to feel fine . . . a man . . .

MAMA   You won't have nothing left then, Walter Lee.

WALTER   (*Coming to her*) I'm going to feel fine, Mama. I'm going to look that son-of-a-bitch in the eyes and say (*He falters*) and say, "All right, Mr. Lindner (*He falters even more*) that's your neighborhood out there. You got the right to keep it like you want. You got the right to have it like you want. Just write the check and—the house is yours." And, and I am going to say (*His voice almost breaks*) and you—you people just put the money in my hand and you won't have to live next to this bunch of stinking niggers! (*He straightens up and moves away from his mother, walking around the room.*) Maybe—maybe I'll just get down on my black knees . . . (*He does so;* RUTH *and* BENNIE *and* MAMA *watch him in frozen horror*) Captain, Mistuh, Bossman. (*He starts crying.*) A-hee-hee-hee! (*Wringing his hands in profoundly anguished imitation*) Yassssssuh! Great White Father, just gi' ussen de money, fo' God's sake, and we's ain't gwine come out deh and dirty up yo' white folks' neighborhood . . . (*He breaks down completely, then gets up and goes into the bedroom.*)

BENEATHA   That is not a man. That is nothing but a toothless rat.

MAMA   Yes—death done come in this here house. (*She is nodding slowly, reflectively.*) Done come walking in my house. On the lips of my children. You what supposed to be my beginning again. You—what supposed to be my harvest. (*To* BENEATHA) You—you mourning your brother?

BENEATHA   He's no brother of mine.

MAMA   What you say?

BENEATHA   I said that that individual in that room is no brother of mine.

MAMA   That's what I thought you said. You feeling like you better than he is today? (BENEATHA *does not answer.*) Yes? What you tell him a minute ago? That he wasn't a man? Yes?

You give him up for me? You done wrote his epitaph too—like the rest of the world? Well, who give you the privilege?

BENEATHA Be on my side for once! You saw what he just did, Mama! You saw him—down on his knees. Wasn't it you who taught me—to despise any man who would do that. Do what he's going to do.

MAMA Yes—I taught you that. Me and your daddy. But I thought I taught you something else too . . . I thought I taught you to love him.

BENEATHA Love him? There is nothing left to love.

MAMA There is always something left to love. And if you ain't learned that, you ain't learned nothing. (*Looking at her*) Have you cried for that boy today? I don't mean for yourself and for the family 'cause we lost the money. I mean for him; what he been through and what it done to him. Child, when do you think is the time to love somebody the most; when they done good and made things easy for everybody? Well then, you ain't through learning—because that ain't the time at all. It's when he's at his lowest and can't believe in hisself 'cause the world done whipped him so. When you starts measuring somebody, measure him right, child, measure him right. Make sure you done taken into account what hills and valleys he come through before he got to wherever he is. (*TRAVIS bursts into the room at the end of the speech, leaving the door open.*)

TRAVIS Grandmama—the moving men are downstairs! The truck just pulled up.

MAMA (*Turning and looking at him*) Are they, baby? They downstairs? (*She sighs and sits.* LINDER *appears in the doorway. He peers in and knocks lightly, to gain attention, and comes in. All turn to look at him.*)

LINDNER (*Hat and briefcase in hand*) Uh—hello. (RUTH *crosses mechanically to the bedroom door and opens it and lets it swing freely and slowly as the lights come up on* WALTER *within, still in his coat, sitting at the far corner of the room. He looks up and out through the room to* LINDNER.)

RUTH He's here. (*A long minute passes, and* WALTER *slowly gets up.*)

LINDNER (*Coming to the table with efficiency, putting his brief-case on the table and starting to unfold papers and unscrew fountain pens*) Well, I certainly was glad to hear from you people. (WALTER *has begun the trek out of the room, slowly and awkwardly, rather like a small boy, passing the back of his sleeve across his mouth from time to time.*) Life can really be so much simpler than people let it be most of the time. Well—with whom do I negotiate? You, Mrs. Younger, or your son here? (MAMA *sits with her hands folded on her lap and her eyes closed as* WALTER *advances.* TRAVIS *goes close to* LINDER *and looks at the papers curiously.*) Just some official papers, sonny.

RUTH Travis, you go downstairs.

MAMA (*Opening her eyes and looking into* WALTER's) No. Travis, you stay right here. And you make him understand what you doing, Walter Lee. You teach him good. Like Willy Harris taught you. You show where our five generations done come to. Go ahead, son.

WALTER (*Looks down into his boy's eyes.* TRAVIS *grins at him merrily and* WALTER *draws him beside him with his arm lightly around his shoulders.*) Well, Mr. Lindner. (BENEATHA *turns away.*) We called you (*There is a profound, simple, groping quality in his speech*) because, well, me and my family (*He looks around and shifts from one foot to the other*), well—we are very plain people . . .

LINDNER Yes—

WALTER I mean—I have worked as a chauffeur most of my life —and my wife here, she does domestic work in people's kitchens. So does my mother. I mean—we are plain people . . .

LINDNER Yes, Mr. Younger—

WALTER (*Really like a small boy, looking down at his shoes and then up at the man*) And—uh—well, my father, well, he was a laborer most of his life.

LINDNER (*Absolutely confused*) Uh, yes—

WALTER (*Looking down at his toes once again*) My father almost beat a man to death once because this man called him a bad name or something, you know what I mean?

LINDNER No, I'm afraid I don't.

WALTER (*Finally straightening up*) Well, what I mean is that we come from people who had a lot of pride. I mean—we are very proud people. And that's my sister over there and she's going to be a doctor—and we are very proud—

LINDNER Well—I am sure that is very nice, but—

WALTER (*Starting to cry and facing the man eye to eye*) What I am telling you is that we called you over here to tell you that we are very proud and that this is—this is my son, who makes the sixth generation of our family in this country, and that we have all thought about your offer and we have decided to move into our house because my father—my father—he earned it. (MAMA *has her eyes closed and is rocking back and forth as though she were in church, with her head nodding the amen yes.*) We don't want to make no trouble for nobody or fight no causes—but we will try to be good neighbors. That's all we got to say. (*He looks the man absolutely in the eyes.*) We don't want your money. (*He turns and walks away from the man.*)

LINDNER (*Looking around at all of them*) I take it then that you have decided to occupy.

BENEATHA That's what the man said.

LINDNER (*To* MAMA *in her reverie*) Then I would like to appeal to you, Mrs. Younger. You are older and wiser and understand things better I am sure . . .

MAMA (*Rising*) I am afraid you don't understand. My son said we was going to move and there ain't nothing left for me to say. (*Shaking her head with double meaning*) You know how these young folks is nowadays, mister. Can't do a thing with 'em. Good-by.

LINDNER (*Folding up his materials*) Well—if you are that final about it . . . There is nothing left for me to say. (*He finishes. He is almost ignored by the family, who are concentrating on* WALTER LEE. *At the door* LINDNER *halts and looks around.*) I sure hope you people know what you're doing. (*He shakes his head and exits.*)

RUTH (*Looking around and coming to life*) Well, for God's sake—if the moving men are here—LET'S GET THE HELL OUT OF HERE!

MAMA (*Into action*) Ain't it the truth! Look at all this here mess. Ruth, put Travis' good jacket on him . . . Walter Lee, fix your tie and tuck your shirt in, you look just like somebody's hoodlum. Lord have mercy, where is my plant? (*She flies to get it amid the general bustling of the family, who are deliberately trying to ignore the nobility of the past moment.*) You all start down . . . Travis child, don't go empty-handed . . . Ruth, where did I put that box with my skillets in it? I want to be in charge of it myself . . . I'm going to make us the biggest dinner we ever ate tonight . . . Beneatha, what's the matter with them stockings? Pull them things up, girl . . . (*The family starts to file out as two moving men appear and begin to carry out the heavier pieces of furniture, bumping into the family as they move about.*)

BENEATHA Mama, Asagai asked me to marry him today and go to Africa—

MAMA (*In the middle of her getting-ready activity*) He did? You ain't old enough to marry nobody (*Seeing the moving men lifting one of her chairs precariously*) Darling, that ain't no bale of cotton, please handle it so we can sit in it again. I had that chair twenty-five years . . . (*The movers sigh with exasperation and go on with their work.*)

BENEATHA (*Girlishly and unreasonably trying to pursue the conversation*) To go to Africa, Mama—be a doctor in Africa . . .

MAMA (*Distracted*) Yes, baby—

WALTER Africa! What he want you to go to Africa for?

BENEATHA To practice there . . .

WALTER   Girl, if you don't get all them silly ideas out your head! You better marry yourself a man with some loot . . .

BENEATHA (*Angrily, precisely as in the first scene of the play*) What have you got to do with who I marry!

WALTER   Plenty. Now I think George Murchison . . . (*He and* BENEATHA *go out yelling at each other vigorously;* BENEATHA *is heard saying that she would not marry* GEORGE MURCHISON *if he were Adam and she were Eve, etc. The anger is loud and real till their voices diminish.* RUTH *stands at the door and turns to* MAMA *and smiles knowingly.*)

MAMA (*Fixing her hat at last*) Yeah—they something all right, my children . . .

RUTH   Yeah—they're something. Let's go, Lena.

MAMA (*Stalling, starting to look around at the house*) Yes, I'm coming. Ruth—

RUTH   Yes?

MAMA (*Quietly, woman to woman*) He finally come into his manhood today, didn't he? Kind of like a rainbow after the rain . . .

RUTH (*Biting her lip lest her own pride explode in front of* MAMA) Yes, Lena. (WALTER's *voice calls for them raucously.*)

MAMA (*Waving* RUTH *out vaguely*) All right, honey—go on down. I be down directly. (RUTH *hesitates, then exits.* MAMA *stands, at last alone in the living room, her plant on the table before her as the lights start to come down. She looks around at all the walls and ceilings and suddenly, despite herself, while the children call below, a great heaving thing rises in her and she puts her fist in her mouth, takes a final desperate look, pulls her coat about her, pats her hat and goes out. The lights dim down. The door opens and she comes back in, grabs her plant, and goes out for the last time.*)

CURTAIN

Scene from
LAND BEYOND THE RIVER
by Loften Mitchell

CHARACTERS

BILL RAIGEN, a tall, husky dark-complexioned man of about thirty-five, good-humored but quick-tempered

DUFF WATERS, forty-five, tall, heavy-set, loud-voiced

J. C. LANGSTON, forty, small, thin, pleasant

THE REVEREND MR. SHELL, a man of medium height, heavily built, stooped from the weight of more than sixty years

REVEREND JOSEPH LAYNE, a tall, thin, bespectacled man with prematurely gray hair, not quite forty, homespun, stubborn

TIME

The recent past

SCENE

A rural county in South Carolina. A school. An evening in March. A group of men have gathered to repair the Jim Crow school. Their music rises through the darkness, then carries under. Now we hear hammers banging against the floor.

I'm going to tell God all my troubles when I get home.
I'm going to tell God all my troubles when I get home
   I'm going to fall down on my knees and pray
   'Cause I wanta meet Him on the Judgment Day.
I'm going to tell God all my troubles when I get home.
I'm going to tell God how you been atreating me when I
                           get home.
I'm going to tell God how you been atreating me when I get
                           home.
   I'm going to set down beside my mother—
   Yes, I'm going to tell it to my sister and brother—
I'm going to tell 'em all about my troubles when I get home.

(*The lights come up.* THE REVEREND MR. SHELL, LAYNE, BILL,
DUFF WATERS, *and* J. C. LANGSTON *are on their knees, pounding
on the floor and singing.*
*The song ends, and the men continue hammering, and hum-
ming. Suddenly,* BILL *brings his hammer down and the wood
splits. He slams down the hammer, springs to his feet.*)

BILL I'm sick of this! Plain sick!

DUFF What's ailing you, boy?

BILL We getting no place. Fast as you hits over yonder, the
wood flies up in my face.

J.C. So you get even. You nail your'n down and it'll fly up in
his face.

BILL That ain't no joke, J.C. This floor's rotten! Some of the
wood that built it musta been on Noah's Ark!

J.C. If you ask me, the Lord wouldn't let Noah use this wood
for his Ark! 'Scuse me, Reverend Layne. 'Scuse me, Reverend
Shell—but if I had this wood around my outhouse it wouldn't
keep a smell inside!

DUFF Negro, you sure talk simple! You expect wood to do
things God Himself can't do.

SHELL   Boys, the name of the Lord, thy God—

LAYNE   I think we ought to work more and talk less.

SHELL   I'm thinking we need some more wood down here, Joe.

J.C.   Watch out 'fore you go through the floor!

DUFF   Man, I ain't that heavy!

J.C.   Damn it, I nailed up that part, and I ain't nailing it up no more tonight. It fall down again and you got to point your big behind at the ceiling and nail it up this time!

DUFF   You just forget the size of my behind.

J.C.   Who the hell can, when it sticks out all over you.

DUFF   Looks better'n your face, else I'd be 'shamed to stand up.

SHELL   Boys, please! Show some respect!

DUFF   Too tired to be showing anything, Reverend Shell. (*Leans back*) Man, I can see me getting to work in the morning. Old Boss Man gonna say: "Duff, you looks bad. Been drinking corn last night, ain't you?" I'm gonna say: "Wish I was, Boss Man, sir, 'cause then I'd have a headache instead of a backache."

J.C.   They tells me you have to have something in your head for it to ache.

DUFF   You shut up, J.C. (*Then*) Come to think of it, I better tell Old Boss Man I was drinking, 'cause if he ever hears who I was working with, it'll be my job for sure.

SHELL   Meaning Layne and me?

DUFF   Ain't calling no names or signifying, Reverend Shell, but all I know is—when I asked for a bank loan last year to fix up my house, the man told me I wasn't getting a Am-I-born-to-die 'cause I belongs to Reverend Layne's church.

J.C.   Ain't no danger of that happening this year 'cause you ain't been to church in so long you'd walk up and knock on the door to get in.

LAYNE   Why didn't you tell us about this before, Duff?

J.C.   Yeah, you could have borrowed off Rev like everybody else did.

DUFF   Them white folks be down on me sure for borrowing off him. He and Reverend Shell ain't worshiped by white folks in these parts—

SHELL   That's the best compliment I've ever been paid.

DUFF   Ain't no compliment. Folks can get real nasty around here. You and Reverend Layne don't hafta count on white folks for your daily bread. You all done burnt the mortgages on your churches.

BILL   All right, boys! What we gonna do?

DUFF   Rest up some.

BILL   I mean, we got to do more'n we doing.

J.C.   Yeah. Let's get started or the roosters'll be crowing 'fore we finish up this floor.

BILL   Sometimes you gets mighty funny when there ain't no joke, J.C.

J.C.   We the joke, arguing when we oughta be working together.

LAYNE   All right, all right. Let's get back to work. (*He starts singing, bangs his hammer to the floor, then notices that no one is singing with him.* DUFF *hits his finger with the hammer, stops, sticks his finger in his mouth. The men all stop working at the same time.*)

SHELL   It's no use—

LAYNE   Rotten through and through.

J.C.   What we gonna do? We've got to fix this floor tonight.

BILL   Why?

LAYNE   Why? Because these children can't be missing one single day of school, that's why.

BILL   Rev, this floor's rotten. Unless we get some new wood down here, somebody's gonna get hurt for sure.

J.C.   Where you gonna get the lumber? School Board sure ain't gonna buy none.

DUFF   There's a whole heap of trees outside.

BILL   You being smart?

LAYNE   Let's try it! At least there'd be something solid down here for tomorrow, and come Saturday we can put down some real lumber.

BILL   You got to be fooling, Reverend.

LAYNE   I'm not! Get your saws and an ax and come on! (*The men look at each other.*) Come on, I said! (*The men pick up their saws, look at them, then at each other.*)

BILL   Talk sense, Reverend! Only thing that'll get them trees down is a electric saw.

SHELL   Anybody know where we can get one?

DUFF   And where we gonna get the electricity after we gets the saw?

J.C.   Yeah. (*They are silent.*) What you gonna do, Reverend Layne?

LAYNE   I don't know. I don't know. (*One by one the men flop on benches or on the floor.*) Guess that wasn't such a good idea.

BILL   What kinda fools are we anyway? Talking about going out there in the night to cut down trees? Don't we pay our taxes for our kids to go to . . .

LAYNE   Bill, please! Just let me think a minute!

DUFF   Oh no! Don't do no more thinking if you gonna come up with another idea like that!

LAYNE   You got any better ones? (*He is sharp and almost instantly sorry for his words. He turns away.* SHELL *goes to*

him, puts his hand on his shoulder. BILL *stands looking at this.*
J.C. *goes to* DUFF.)

J.C. You oughta be shamed of yourself, Duff Waters.

DUFF Didn't mean no harm, Reverend. Honest—

J.C. You did so!

DUFF Don't tell me what I meant!

J.C. You just trying to get outta doing any more work around
here. Work is your father's name and you don't believe in
hitting him a lick!

DUFF You a dirty liar!

J.C. Pat your foot while I play it! (*Angrily*) Pick on me, you
big ox! Betcha I'll take you down a button hole lower!
(DUFF *grabs* J.C. *by the collar, lifts him into the air.* BILL
rushes between them, pushes them apart.)

BILL Oh, shut up, both of you!

DUFF (*To* BILL) Who you shoving?

BILL *You*, damn it!

SHELL Boys, for heaven's sake!

J.C. Yeah. Break it up! (*Steps between* BILL *and* DUFF. *As he
steps between them,* J.C. *steps on* DUFF's *foot.* DUFF *lets out a
yell, grabs his foot.*)

DUFF You stepped on my toe, you little son-of-a- (*Before* DUFF
can finish, J.C. *has rushed into him and hit him. They clench
and* DUFF *wrestles* J.C. *to the floor.* BILL *stands off at one side
and begins to laugh at them.* SHELL *and* LAYNE *rush to try to
pull* DUFF *off* J.C.)

LAYNE Bill! Bill! (BILL *feigns ignorance. While* LAYNE *is talking,* DUFF *continues working on* J.C. BILL *finally pulls* DUFF *off*
J.C. DUFF *strikes* BILL *accidentally.* BILL *loses his temper, strikes*
DUFF *back.* SHELL *and* LAYNE *are busy trying to break up this
free for all.* LAYNE *has grabbed* BILL *by now and* SHELL *is
holding* J.C. DUFF *turns on* J.C. *and declares:*)

DUFF You started this, you— (*And* DUFF *draws back, swings at* J.C. J.C. *ducks and* DUFF *strikes* SHELL. SHELL *loses his temper and yells:*)

SHELL You damn fool! (*He raises his hand to strike back, then he remembers his religion.*) Lord, forgive me! (DUFF *is shocked at hearing the old preacher curse. He stands there with both hands in the air.* J.C. *seizes the opportunity. He springs into* DUFF, *strikes him in the belly.* DUFF *doesn't budge. Now,* DUFF *throws a wild haymaker.* J.C. *ducks again. The momentum of* DUFF's *swing carries him to the floor. At this very moment,* LAYNE *calls out:*)

LAYNE Jesus, God! It's wrong—wrong!

SHELL Layne—

LAYNE It is wrong I tell you—working on floors that aren't floors, spilling your blood over them for nothing! God knows it's a sin!

SHELL Joe, please . . .

BILL He's right. It is a sin and a shame, Reverend Shell. I'm saying we oughta burn down the whole shebang!

J.C. Sure right! That's one way of getting a new schoolhouse!

DUFF I'll sure give you a match.

LAYNE I will not have you down here another night like this! May I go to my grave this moment if I do! How you gonna be separate and equal at the same time?

SHELL I don't know that, but I know the state law.

LAYNE This school is separate, all right, but it sure ain't equal.

BILL Dad-blame it, I pay my taxes to keep that law in business. We oughta sue 'em to make it work! (*Sees* DUFF *packing tools.*) What you say, Duff.

DUFF My name is Fess, I ain't in this mess.

LAYNE What does that mean?

DUFF It means, I got to live out there with them white folks, and I aims to live. Soon as old white man says "Boo" to 'em they gonna start backing up! And I ain't gonna have my toes around for 'em to back up on!

LAYNE It won't just be one or two of us suing. We're going to have to get a whole heap of names on some kind of petition, authorizing Ben Ellis and his organization to represent us in court.

SHELL For the bus case, we only needed one.

LAYNE This is different. If it's only one or two, somebody might move away or withdraw—

DUFF Or get killed.

LAYNE Or get killed.

J.C. We can take all the hell they wanta give us!

BILL Yeah, ain't nobody here looking for no picnic! A body can die but once and it might as well be for something like this.

DUFF I ain't said a word against it.

LAYNE (*Looks up*) "Out of darkness have I cried unto thee, O Lord! Lord hear my prayer." If any soul has to die in this, let it be me! Let it be me!

SHELL It won't be just you, J.C. It'll be all of us. Now is the time! Now is the time to shout in righteous indignation!

BILL Every last one of us.

SHELL (*Begins to hum "Oh, Freedom." Others pick it up.*)
Oh, Freedom! Oh, Freedom!
Oh, Freedom over me!
And before I'll be a slave,
I'll be buried in my grave,
And go home to my Lord and be free!
(*They are singing courageously. They continue to sing as they get their things and start for home.*)

*　　*　　*

Scene from
DAY OF ABSENCE
by Douglas Turner Ward

THE TIME is now, in an unnamed southern town of medium population.

CHARACTERS

> ANNOUNCER
>
> THE MAYOR
>
> TOWNSPEOPLE
>
> Characters are played in white-face. Mayor wears a white seersucker ensemble, ten-gallon hat, red string tie, and blue belt.

SCENE

> *Lights come up on Huntley-Brinkley-Murrow-Sevareid-Cronkite-Reasoner-type Announcer grasping a hand-held microphone (imaginary).*

ANNOUNCER Ladies and gentlemen, as you trudge in from the joys and headaches of workday chores and dusk begins to descend on this sleepy southern hamlet, we *repeat*—today —before early morning dew had dried upon magnolia blossoms, your comrade citizens of this lovely Dixie village awoke to the realization that some—pardon me!—not some but *all of their Negroes* were missing . . . absent, vamoosed, departed, at bay, fugitive, away, gone and so-far unretrieved. We take you now to offices of the one man into whose hands has been thrust the final responsibility of rescuing this shuddering metropolis from the precipice of destruction . . . We give you the honorable Mayor, Henry R. E. Lee . . . Hello, Mayor Lee.

MAYOR (*Jovially*) Hello, Jack.

ANNOUNCER Mayor Lee, we have just concluded interviews with some of your city's leading spokesmen. If I may say so, sir, they don't sound too encouraging about the situation.

MAYOR Nonsense, Jack! The situation's well in hand as it could be under the circumstances. Couldn't be better in hand. Underneath every dark cloud, Jack, there's always a ray of sunlight, ha, ha, ha.

ANNOUNCER Have you discovered one, sir?

MAYOR Well, Jack, I'll tell you . . . Of course we've been faced wit' a little crisis, but look at it like this—we've faced 'em befo': Sherman marched through Georgia—*once!* Lincoln freed the slaves—*momentarily!* Carpetbaggers even put Nigras in the Governor's mansion, state legislature, Congress and the Senate of the United States. But what happened?—Ole Dixie bounced right on back up. . . . At this moment the Supreme Court's trying to put Nigras in our schools and the Nigra has got it in his haid to put hisself everywhere. . . . But what you 'spect go'n' happen?—Ole Dixie will kangaroo back even higher. Southern courage, fortitude, chivalry, and superiority always wins out. . . . *Shucks!* We'll have us some Nigras befo' daylight is gone!

ANNOUNCER   Mr. Mayor, I hate to introduce this note, but in an earlier interview, one of your chief opponents, Mr. Clan, hinted at your own complicity in the affair—

MAYOR   *A lot of Poppycock!* Clan is politicking! I've beaten him four times outta four and I'll beat him four more times outta four! This is not time for partisan politics! What we need now is level-headedness and across-the-board unity. This typical, rash, mealy-mouth, shooting-off-at-the-lip of Clan and his ilk proves their insincerity and voters will remember that in the next election! Won't you, voters?! (*Has risen to the height of campaign oratory*)

ANNOUNCER   Mr. Mayor! . . . Mr. Mayor! . . . Please—

MAYOR   —I tell you, I promise you—

ANNOUNCER   PLEASE, MR. MAYOR!

MAYOR   Huh? . . . Oh—yes, carry on.

ANNOUNCER   Mr. Mayor, your cheerfulness and infectious good spirits lead me to conclude that startling new developments warrant fresh-found optimism. What concrete, declassified information do you have to support your claim that Negroes will reappear before nightfall?

MAYOR   *Me—that's what! Me!* A personal appeal from *me!* Directly to them! . . . Although we wouldn't let 'em march to the polls and express their affection for me through the ballot box, we've always known I'm held highest in their esteem. A direct address from their beloved Mayor! . . . If they's anywheres close within the sound of my voice, they'll shape up! Or let us know by a sign they's ready to!

ANNOUNCER   I'm delighted to offer our network's facilities for such a crucial public interest address, sir.

MAYOR   Thank you, I'm very grateful . . . Good evening . . . Despite the fact that millions of you wonderful people throughout the nation are viewing and listening to this momentous broadcast—and I thank you for your concern and sympathy in this hour of our peril—I primarily want to con-

centrate my attention and address these remarks solely for
the benefit of our departed Nigra friends who may be listening
somewheres in our farflung land to the sound of my voice.
. . . If you are—it is with heartfelt emotion and fond memories
of our happy association that I ask—"Where are you . . . ?"
Your absence has left a void in the bosom of every single man,
woman, and child of our great city. I tell you, you don't
know what it means for us to wake up in the morning and
discover that your cheerful, grinning, happy-go-lucky faces
are missing! . . . From the depths of my heart, I can only
humbly suggest what it means to me personally. You see, the
one face I will never be able to erase from my memory is
the face, not of my Ma, not of Pa, neither wife or child,
but the image of the first woman I came to love so well when
just a wee lad, the vision of the first human I laid clear sight
on at childbirth, the profile—better yet, the full face of my
dear old—Jemimah—God rest her soul—Yes! My dear ole
mammy, wit' her round ebony moonbeam gleaming down upon
me in the crib, teeth shining, blood-red bandana standing
starched, peaked and proud, gazing down upon me affection-
ately as she crooned me a southern lullaby—oh! It's a memora-
ble picture I will eternally cherish in permanent treasure
chambers of my heart, now and forever always. . . . Well, if
this radiant image can remain so infinitely vivid to me all
these many years after her unfortunate demise in the po' folks'
home—think of the misery the rest of us must be suffering
after being freshly denied your soothing presence?! We need
ya. If you kin hear me, just contact this station 'n' I will
welcome you back personally. Let me just tell you that since
you eloped, nothing has been the same. How could it? You're
part of us, you belong to us. Just give us a sign and we'll be
contented that all is well. . . . Now if you've skipped away
on a little fun-fest, we understand, ha, ha. We know you like
a good time and we don't begrudge it to ya. Hell—er, er, we
like a good time ourselves—who doesn't? In fact, think of all
the good times we've had together, huh? We've had some
real fun, you and us, yesiree! Nobody knows better than you
and I what fun we've had together. You singing us those old
southern coon songs and dancing those Nigra jigs and us

clapping, prodding 'n' spurring you on! Lots of fun, huh?!
Oh boy! The times we've had together. If you've snucked
away for a bit of fun by yourself, we'll go 'long wit' ya—
long as you let us know where you at so we won't be worried
about you. We'll go 'long wit' you long as you don't take
the joke too far. I'll admit a joke is a joke and you've
played a *lulu!* I'm warning you, we can't stand much more
horsing 'round from you! Business is business 'n' fun is fun!
You've had your fun so now let's get down to business! Come
on back, *you hear me!!!* If you been hoodwinked by agents
of some foreign government, I've been authorized by the Pres-
ident of the United States to inform you that this liberty-loving
Republic is prepared to rescue you from their clutches. Don't
pay no 'tention to their sireeen songs and atheistic promises!
You better off under our control and you know it! If you been
bamboozled by rabble-rousing nonsense of your own so-called
leaders, we prepared to offer some protection. Just call us up!
Just give us a sign! Come on, give us a sign—give us a sign
—even a teeny-weeny one . . . ??!! (*Glances around, checking
on possible communications. A bevy of headshakes indicate no
success.* MAYOR *returns to address with desperate fervor.*)
Now look—you don't know what you doing! If you persist
in this disobedience, you know all too well the consequences!
We'll track you to the end of the earth, beyond the galaxy,
across the stars! We'll capture you and chastise you with all
the vengeance we command! 'N' you know only too well how
stern we kin be when double-crossed! The city, the state, and
the entire nation will crucify you for this unpardonable
defiance! (*Checks again*) No call . . . ? No sign . . . ? Time
is running out! Deadline slipping past! They gotta respond!
They gotta! (*Resuming*) Listen to me! I'm begging y'all,
you've gotta come back . . . ! *Look, George!* (*Waves dirty
rag aloft*) I brought the rag you wax the car wit' . . . Don't
this bring back memories, George, of all the days you spent
shining that automobile to shimmering perfection . . . ? And
you, Rufus?! Here's the shoe polisher and the brush! . . .
'Member, Rufus?! . . . Remember the happy mornings you
spent popping this rag and whisking this brush so furiously
till it created music that was symphonee to the ear . . . ?

And you—*Mandy?* . . . Here's the waste-basket you didn't dump this morning. I saved it just for you! . . . *Look,* all y'all out there . . . ? (*Signals, and a three-person procession parades one after the other before the imaginary camera.* DOLL WOMAN—MOP MAN—BRUSH MAN)

DOLL WOMAN (*Brandishing a crying baby [doll] as she strolls past and exits*) She's been crying ever since you left, Caldonia . . .

MOP MAN (*Flashing mop*) It's been waiting in the same corner, Buster . . .

BRUSH MAN (*Flagging toilet brush in one hand and toilet plunger in other*) It's been dry ever since you left, Washington . . .

MAYOR (*Jumping in on the heels of the last exit*) Don't these things mean anything to y'all? By God! Are your memories so short?! Is there nothing sacred to ya? Please come back, for my sake, please! All of you—even you questionable ones! I promise no harm will be done to you! Revenge is disallowed! We'll forgive everything! Just come on back and I'll git down on my knees. (*Immediately drops to knees*) I'll be kneeling in the middle of Dixie Avenue to kiss the first shoe of the first one 'a you to show up. . . . I'll smooch any other spot you request. . . . Erase this nightmare 'n' we'll concede any demand you make, just come on back—please???!! . . . *pleeeeeeeze?!!!*

VOICE (*Shouting*) Time!!!

MAYOR (*Remaining on knees, frozen in a pose of supplication. After a brief, deadly silence he whispers almost inaudibly.*) They wouldn't answer . . .

BLACKOUT

Scene from
NATURAL MAN
by Theodore Browne

A play based on the legend of John Henry

TIME   The early 1880s

CHARACTERS

> CONGREGATION members
> The PREACHER
> JOHN HENRY

SCENE

> *A camp-meeting. A small band of worshipers are seated on benches facing a crude, makeshift pulpit, from which a portly preacher exhorts them to worship. There are two rows of benches, with a narrow aisle between them. The meeting is well under way as the lights come up, and there is an all-pervading air of unrestrained religious fervor, as the* CONGREGATION, *led by the* PREACHER, *sing* "Shine on Me."

CONGREGATION
  Shine on me,
  Lord, shine on me.
  I wants de light from de lighthouse,
  To shine on me.
  Shine on me,
  Lord, shine on me,
  I wants de light from de lighthouse
  To shine on me.
  *There are incidental cries and murmurs of, "Praise be de
  Lord!" "Have mercy, Lord!" "Blessed Saviour!" etc., as the
  song is being sung. Some of the members stand and sway to
  the rhythm, clapping their hands and patting their feet.*

PREACHER (*As the* CONGREGATION *relax softly into a humming of
  the song. He speaks out over this, giving to his voice a sort of
  mournful, heartfelt quality.*) Open up your troubled hearts to
  Jesus. Don't wait too long, sisters and brothers. Don't wait till
  you sick and on your dying bed to call to Him. Oh, sisters
  and brothers, we never know when Ole Death gwine snatch
  us way. Sometimes Death creeps up on the sinner-man when
  he ain't expecting him. Sometimes he overtakes the weary
  traveler, a long ways from home. You might be working in
  the field. He might come to you while you lost in slumber. Ole
  Death's a mighty reaper.

CONGREGATION Amen, Glory Hallelujah! Do, Jesus!

PREACHER Ole Death ain't got no shame. He walks the troubled
  waters of the sea and the ocean. He visits the rich and the
  poor. He stretches out his arms and spreads pestilence and
  destruction throughout the land.

CONGREGATION Yes, he do, Preacher! Death's a mighty man!

PREACHER Oh, brothers and sisters, don't you want Jesus to walk
  with you, through all your trials and tribulations, through the
  valley of the shadow of death?

CONGREGATION Yes, Jesus! Oh, my Jesus!

OLD WOMAN *(Rises and starts to sing, the whole* CONGREGATION *joining in, swaying and moaning.)*
I wants Jesus to walk with me,
I wants Jesus to walk with me,
Whilst I'm on my pilgrim's journey,
I wants Jesus to walk with me.

PREACHER Don't you want Jesus to talk with you?

CONGREGATION Yes, Jesus! *(A young girl rises, filled with religious fervor, and shouts as she walks up the aisle to the pulpit, "Save my soul, Jesus! Don't let me sin no more!" She kneels before the pulpit, face buried in her hands, and weeps.)*

OLD WOMAN
I wants Jesus to talk with me,
I wants Jesus to talk with me,
Whilst I'm on my pilgrim's journey
I wants Jesus to talk with me.

PREACHER Don't you want Jesus to comfort you?

CONGREGATION Yes, Jesus! Comfort me, Lord!

OLD WOMAN
I wants Jesus to comfort me,
I wants Jesus to comfort me,
Whilst I'm on my pilgrim's journey,
I wants Jesus to comfort me
(Her voice cracked and full of grief, she gives her testimonial.)
Jesus, have mercy on my boy wherever he is tonight. I wants you to walk with him, Jesus. He left home, his heart troubled and hurt. Ain't there something you can do for him, Jesus? I'm just a lone, old woman and all my days is numbered and short. I won't be here long, Lord. Maybe I won't never see my boy's face again in this life, Lord. But, wherever he is to-night, won't you go to him and just tell him that his ole mammy's praying for his soul? Tell him that his ole mammy forgives all he's ever done. Take the grief out of his heart, Jesus. Tell him tain't right to gamble and drink and keep bad company. Tell him that the sinner-life ain't the life his ole mammy wants him to lead. Thank you, Jesus, thank you!
(She sits down, her head bowed.)

PREACHER (*As the* CONGREGATION *hums*) Bless your heart, sister. Bless the hearts of the mothers who got sons that strayed a long ways from home.

CONGREGATION Amen, Hallelujah!

PREACHER That's fallen by the wayside.

CONGREGATION Oh, my Jesus! By the wayside!

PREACHER Mothers whose boys is weary travelers 'long the dark and stormy highway.

CONGREGATION Dark and stormy highway! Bless em, Lord!

PREACHER Bless them lonely sinners, whose hearts may be troubled with the griefs of sorrow. Guide them, Oh, Heavenly Father, in the paths of righteousness. (*The singing resumes. As it attains a climactic fervor, the ragged and mud-begrimed figure of* JOHN HENRY *appears at the rear of the church. His appearance bespeaks of days of hardships encountered while hiding in the swampland after his escape from the prison chain-gang.*) Come forward, brother. Is your heart troubled? (JOHN HENRY *walks slowly up the aisle, there there is a lull and the faces of the worshipers are taut with fear and wonderment.*)

JOHN HENRY (*Head bowed, his voice trembles as he speaks slowly.*) Yes, Preacher, my heart's troubled. I been standing outside listening to your sermon and to what the old lady say 'bout her son. So I made up my mind to come inside. I wasn't aiming to at first. I figgered, maybe, you all wouldn't want me round.

PREACHER You's in the house of the Lord, brother. I don't know as whether I remembers seeing you 'round here before.

JOHN HENRY No, you ain't never seen me before.

PREACHER My name is Reverend Jones—Elder Jones, as most folks calls me. (*Shakes hands with* JOHN HENRY, *who carries in the other hand the shotgun he took from the guard*)— Glad to have you, brother—. I'm sorry, you didn't tell me your name.

JOHN HENRY Jes' call me "brother," 'cause who I is ain't nobody's business. (*Partly to the* CONGREGATION *and partly to the* PREACHER) I ain't saying I'm no true Christian and I ain't saying I'm no sinner-man. I only know that I'm natural-born. I had a mother that birthed me, but long time ago, 'fore I gits in trouble, my mother, she was laid to rest in the lonesome graveyard, 'neath the oak trees and the sleeping willows. She's gone on up to Glory. And I been walking the earth by myself ever since. Ain't no man living or dead I ever mistreated. But I gits in a mess of trouble and they shackle my feet . . . with a ball and chain, and took my rights away. But I done my work, till the white guard on the chain-gang started messing up with me, and make me mad, then I—I killed him stone dead and make my gitaway.

PREACHER (*Terrified*) You ain't oughta come here, brother!

JOHN HENRY Where else could I come to?

PREACHER You liable to git us all in trouble!

CONGREGATION We can't help no convict! White folks kill us all! We's God-fearing people!

JOHN HENRY (*Despairing*) I had to come to somebody, Preacher. I ain't got a friend in the world. Six weeks all by myself, in the dismal swamps and not a soul to talk to, nearbout drive me 'stracted. Cain't you tell me what to do? Cain't any of you all God-fearing Christians tell me what to do?

PREACHER (*Regains a definite composure, then speaks benignly*) There's two kinds of laws, Brother. There's the law of man and there's the law of God. (*This receives the Amen sanctions of the* CONGREGATION.) And we mortal folks is jedged by both of them laws. Go on back to the chain gang and give yourself up and be jedged by the law of man. Then the law of God will be your next jedge.

CONGREGATION Amen, Preacher, Amen!

JOHN HENRY Be no need for God time them white folks git done judging me!

PREACHER The world, my brother, ain't made for the natural man. God, he ain't 'round to protect you no more. God's turnt his back on this sinful world. Washed his hands clean of Adam and Adam's breed. Brother, you's hemmed in by four walls of solid earth. Brother, you cain't break through 'em. So heed me when I tells you, turn the other cheek! Yea, yea! Praise God! Git humble! Pray! Git meek! Meek as the lamb! For the Lawd say, Blessed is the meek for they shall inherit the earth and the kingdom to come! (*Amens from the* CONGREGA-TION)—Pray, brother! Pray! Git down low . . . low . . . low! (*As if struck down by some unseen power,* JOHN HENRY *falls to his knees.*) . . . Repent ye, saith the Lawd! (*Confused, fear-ridden,* JOHN HENRY *makes an effort to pray—"get his soul right"—shaking his head like a drunken man. The* CON-GREGATION *are gathered about him, singing with fervor, "Shine on Me" . . . etc.*)

JOHN HENRY (*Suddenly rises and cries out . . . unregenerate and savagely*) Cain't do it! I ain't got nothing 'ginst the Almighty's laws and ruling, but I ain't letting no manmade laws rule over me!

WORSHIPER You gwine bring trouble to all we black folks!

OLD WOMAN (*As* JOHN HENRY *turns to leave*) Wait a minute, son. Where you aiming to go?

JOHN HENRY I cain't say. All I know is I'm catching the first freight train that comes along. Going where I can make some hard-earned money and spend it as I please. Enjoy life, that's what I'm going to do! Maybe I run cross that son of yours where I'm going. I'll tell him what you say—to pray and walk with Jesus. (*He laughs out loud.*) Say, why don't you jes' have me tell that his old mammy loves the ground he walks on and she ain't caring what he does? Maybe he ain't bad like you thinks. Maybe he's jes' natural-born, like me. Cain't live like you and the preacher want him to. Maybe he jes cain't bow his head and walk humble. You got to let him be . . . (*To the* PREACHER) Well, Preacher, before I go, I want to leave something with you for the church. I ain't got no money. This all I got. This all I got. This shotgun. (*Hands the gun to the* PREACHER *who stares at him and the gun in utter bewilderment*) You keep it, 'cause I won't be needing this old musket any more! (*Freight train whistle blows.* JOHN HENRY *hears it, gives a knowing look at the bewildered* PREACHER *and to the* CONGREGATION . . . *and is on his way. Suddenly a worshiper jumps to his feet and commences to sing. The whole* CONGREGATION *and the* PREACHER *are swept away by spiritual abandon.*)

CONGREGATION

This train don't carry no liars, this train.
This train don't carry no liars, this train . . .

JOHN HENRY (*Shouting over the* CONGREGATION *and* PREACHER, *his voice rising, lyrical, eloquent*) . . . I'm as free as the Blue Ridge Mountain, the Mississippi River, the Tall Lonesome Pine! Like them, I leaves something of myself behind when I goes. My spirit's in all of you. You my spirit reaching up outta the earth. Great God-A-Mighty, what would it be like if all the natural foks was to reach up at the same time? They could reach to high heaven and ease it down to earth! (CONGREGATION *keeps singing, trying to shout out the sound of his voice as* JOHN HENRY *runs out into the night.*)

❈   ❈   ❈

Scene from

THE AFRICAN GARDEN

by Alice Childress

TIME   One summer day . . . at the tail-end of a riot (mid-1960's)

PLACE   Harlem, U.S.A.

CHARACTERS

SIMON, a boy about ten years old
ASHLEY, a *man,* but definitely

SCENE   A kitchen—in an apartment.

(SIMON *enters, places a large paper bag on the table. The entrance to the apartment is through the kitchen. There is a knock on the door.*)

SIMON Who is it?

ASHLEY (*Off stage*) Mr. Ashley.

SIMON (*Tries to place paper sack in the refrigerator, but the package is too large to fit inside. He frantically searches for a place to put it . . . finally puts it back on the table.*) Who? Whatcha say?

ASHLEY (*Off stage*) You got a room for rent?

SIMON Just a minute . . . a minute . . . (*He opens the door, but the safety chain is still fastened.*) Say what?

ASHLEY Huh?

SIMON I say . . . whatcha want?

ASHLEY I understand you got a room for rent.

SIMON Yessir. (*He opens the door.* ASHLEY *enters carrying a battered, much-traveled piece of luggage.* SIMON *clears one of the kitchen chairs of magazines and papers. The kitchen is clean but very mixed up, things out of place, dishes from breakfast still in evidence on the table etc.*) Have a seat. My . . . my . . . mother, not home from work yet. She work downtown in a big hotel doin' what you call chambermaid. House was suppose to be straight fore anybody get here . . . but I was busy . . . just got here myself. Have a seat.

ASHLEY The riot really hit this block hard.

SIMON Oh, I don't know, the block jus' be lookin' like that anyway. (*Self-consciously studying the paper bag and wondering what to do with it.*) You can wait till Mama get here . . . or go and then come back . . . or whatever.

ASHLEY (*Glancing at the bag and noticing the boy's confusion*) You been looting in the stores?

SIMON No . . . no, sir.

ASHLEY Looks like it.

SIMON   A man give me this meat . . . but he wasn't lootin'. That's the kind of business he's in all the time.

ASHLEY   Hmmmmmmm, he's a butcher?

SIMON   No sir, he's a . . . he's a . . . I don' know.

ASHLEY   (*Resting his suitcase*)   Look-a-here, boy, I don't carry no tales, so you can trust me. A man's word is his word, okay?

SIMON   Okay. (*The boy tears the bag open and displays a huge package of meat for Ashley's inspection.*)

ASHLEY   Great googa-mooga. Steaks, chops, chicken, and frank-footers.

SIMON   The man who give it to me is a cattle rustler. A cattle rustler is a man who cops meat outta the supermarket.

ASHLEY   Why did you say he wasn't lootin?

SIMON   I wasn't . . . and he wasn't either. He just be roundin' up meat like that every day when they ain't even any riot. That's his regular business . . . and he sell it for half price and that way people can ford to eat steak and lamb chops and . . .

ASHLEY   Why did he give it to you?

SIMON   I don' know. He walk up to me an my friend, Carter, and he say . . . "You boys divide this govmint-branded cattle . . . and eat till you bust . . . someday you can maybe do somethin for me.

ASHLEY   That's the stuff you got to watch. Don' let nobody buy you or sell you.

SIMON   My mother not gonna believe anybody jus give me all-a this. But it sure be a terrible waste to throw it out.

ASHLEY   Sure would.

SIMON   I know. Why don't you tell her that you brought it for us.

ASHLEY   No, I can't do that for you. Put it away before it spoils. (ASHLEY *helps* SIMON *put the meat in the refrigerator as they continue talking.*) Tell her what you told me. She'll give you a good talkin to . . . then yall can eat the steak.

SIMON You don' know her. She'd throw it away, I do believe. Maybe I could give it back to Old Soldier . . . but . . . but . . .

ASHLEY Well, you didn't mean to tell his name. That comes from your mouth speakin before your mind thinks. Old Soldier, huh?

SIMON He not so old, but he was in World War Two . . . and that's what he say alla time . . . "I'm a *old* soldier." He always hittin' on a new supermarket so nobody get to know his face too regular. He buy sugar and a sack-a potatoes . . . and maybe toilet paper . . . and pay for alla that. But underneath his coat he be rustlin steaks. Might be four or five at a haul . . .

ASHLEY And you think that's smart, dontcha?

SIMON No, sir.

ASHLEY What's your name, boy?

SIMON Simon. Simple Simon . . . they say that in school. Simon Brown . . . what's yours?

ASHLEY M. D. Ashley. Everybody calls me Ashley . . . or Mr. Ashley. You know what the M. stands for? *Maytag* . . . how 'bout that? That's worse than Simon. Down home, in the back country . . . my folks couldn't read. Come time to make out a birth certificate . . . they look round maybe the kitchen . . . and copy any name they see off-a the calendar or the stove. My papa copied down *Maytag* off the washin' machine . . . and *Diamond* . . . from a box-a matches. Ashley was the name-a his grandpa's slave master . . . so there's my name— Maytag Diamond Ashley.

SIMON It sound good though. Mister Maytag Diamond Ashley.

ASHLEY They got to callin me "Doc" because-a the M. D. initials.

SIMON I got a middle name too . . . but I leave it out most-a the time. Simon *T*. Brown. T stand for Turnbo, Simon Turnbo Brown. Turnbo is the name of my mother's stepfather . . . Turnbo Brown.

ASHLEY   Turnbo . . . sounds like a name you might find on a good farm tractor.

SIMON   Yessir.

ASHLEY   Turnbo Brown . . . Simon Turnbo Brown. Your name is the same as your step-grandfather's?

SIMON   Yessir. He down in Mississippi. My mother say he was so kind to everybody. He treat my mama like she was his own child and not a step . . . she say he treat her better than some do their own. She put Simon on because her mother always had wish for a son to name Simon . . . after a man name Simon-call-Peter . . . which is in the Bible.

ASHLEY   Boy, that is something to be proud of . . . you named by and for your grandparent.

SIMON   That right?

ASHLEY   Shows you come from a long line-a people. Course everybody did, when you come to think of it. But you're at least a third- or fourth-generation Brown. Simon Turnbo Brown . . . of the Browns of Mississippi and New York.

SIMON   And Grandpa Brown got a brother who lives in Detroit, Michigan.

ASHLEY   Oh, well, great googa-mooga, you're Simon Turnbo Brown of Mississippi, Michigan, *and* New York. Simon T. Brown, Esquire. A gentleman, a man of importance.

SIMON   (*Admiring the way his name is spoken*)   You kiddin.

ASHLEY   And when you're a man, you'll be a man of importance whether you use the Esquire or not. (SIMON *begins to straighten up the kitchen.*)

SIMON   A boy in my class is named Abdul. He's a Muslim . . . and his folks changed their name from Jackson, cause they say it was a slave name . . . and no African was ever name Jackson.

ASHLEY That's very true. And I know a guy who named himself Chaka cause Chaka was the name of a great Zulu Warrior. This fella told me that no African had a Muslim name till they were converted and brought into the Nation of Islam by the Mohammedans of North Africa.

SIMON That right? You just don't know what to think, huh?

ASHLEY Yeah, there's a awful lotta bags out here to be jumped in when we ready to jump. But Simon, Abdul and Chaka gonna have to get together somehow and make everything all right. Fortunately, I get along with Africans, Afro-Americans, Colored people, Negroes, Blacks . . . and also even with some niggers, cause it's to my best interest. Boy, let me help you straighten up this kitchen. When your house is mixed up . . . it shows that your mind is confused.

SIMON That right? I thought *your* name might be Abdul cause you don't gas your hair . . . and look like not even any grease on it.

ASHLEY Right. That's just plain, old, natural, African bush. I used to gas it, but I put that down. Used to gas it and finger-wave it . . . Boy, so many waves it make you seasick. And shiny! Shiny and slick. When a fly light on it . . . he'd fall down and break his leg. Night and day, I was tyin it down, combin' it, lookin at it, gassed, with one big wave and a dip runnin straight cross the toppa my head. Fellas I knew started goin' "natural" and naggin' me bout doing the same. But you can't talk a man into makin a change . . . He's gotta feel changed . . . gotta be your own change . . . otherwise you just jumpin cause they say jump. One day I got to feelin' this was me . . . "naturally me" . . . and then it was.

SIMON Abdul say if you gas your hair it mean you don't like yourself.

ASHLEY Ain't always so. Some folks don't like themselves gassed or ungassed. If you really don't like yourself . . . you can do what you want with your hair . . . and you still won't like yourself. Your mind has to go natural while you straighten your soul . . . the process got to be on the inside. Some-a my best buddies still gas and they like themselves and me too. I don't tell them how they should and oughta look cause that's not to my best interest. They might go from here to the grave with gassed heads . . . but we got other things in common.

SIMON   I know, you mean we all Black.

ASHLEY   No, boy, I mean we all in trouble . . . terrible trouble, and we ain't in it in no bits, pieces, or sections. It's a common trouble, share and share alike, want to or not; the high and the low of us, the rich and the poor of us, the black and the yaller of us, the gas head and the natural bush, the Negro and the Black man, the dungarees and the African robe, the fat black lady with the blow-hair, and the long brown lady in the wig. You and me and your mama and your stepgrandpa . . . the Ph.D. and the high school dropout . . . we in some terrible deep trouble . . . and we in it together.

SIMON   You a fine speechmaker, but who's right? What's the right thing to do or not to do? Tell me who is right.

ASHLEY   Keep workin', work and talk. If there was just a plain, straight right and wrong to everything . . . a sort of ABC of life . . . all we'd have to do is write a rule book . . . and you could wake up in the mornin' and follow the rules in your little book all day long. But life keeps twistin' and turnin', what is so today ain't so tomorrow, nothin' stands still for you. Keep workin'. Boy, where's your dustcloth? Life is like . . . well, we can't stop you from growin', can we?

SIMON   No, that's somethin we can't help, also I *want* to grow. Mama say I might be small-built cause lotsa her folks was . . . but I wanta be tall.

ASHLEY   But a man is a man . . . be he flyweight or heavyweight, a man is a man. I don't wish to be tall, short, light, dark, keen-featured or heavy-featured . . . cause I am what I am . . . but I do wanta be free . . . and I'm gonna be . . . by any means possible . . . and you just better-black-believe-it.

SIMON   Oh, please rent the room. Maytag Diamond Ashley . . . I want you to live here. It's awful small but you can stay in the kitchen a lot . . . and the rent is only eight-fifty a week, eight if you don't cook. If I was grown and payin' the rent myself, I'd let you stay here for free. You the only grownup I ever met who just *talk* to me like I'm some other person. All grownups say . . . "How old are you? That's nice." What's so nice 'bout how old you are? You got nothin' to do with that at all. Then they say . . . "Study your lesson so you can be somebody." Everybody is somebody even if they just a wino. Then they say . . . "How is the school?" Ain't that a question? The school is fine . . . it just standin' there bein' a school. But how is Simon Turnbo Brown? Please take the room. This is it right in here. (*Opens door to room off kitchen*)

ASHLEY   (*Peeps in room, then sighs*)   It is small. I'd have to back in to lay on the bed. But . . . I'll take it, my friend, if your mama wants me.

SIMON   She will, I know she will!

❖   ❖   ❖

BIOGRAPHIES

FLOYD BARBOUR grew up in Washington, D.C. He is a graduate of Bowdoin College in Brunswick, Maine, and is currently teaching courses in Black literature at M.I.T. and Boston University. He is the author of several plays which have been performed at Yale University, Howard University, Brandeis University and The Institute for Advanced Studies in the Theatre Arts. He recently completed a long play and is now at work on a novel. Barbour is a fine editor and has compiled one anthology, *The Black Power Revolt* published by Porter Sargent of Boston, and is preparing a second, *The Black Seventies*. He makes his home in Boston. The apparent gentleness of his work is as subtle as a sheathed blade.

WILLIAM B. BRANCH playwright, journalist and film producer, born in New Haven, Connecticut, is a graduate of Northwestern University, and holds an M.A. degree from Columbia. His first play was *A Medal for Willie*, produced in a Harlem Cabaret Theatre for a six-week run. Since then he has turned out many plays for theatre and television. Among them are *In Splendid Error*, a historical drama about John Brown and Frederick Douglass; *A Wreath for Udomo*, presented on the London stage and based upon Peter Abrahams' prophetic novel about the rise and fall of an African prime minister; *Light in the Southern Sky*, an NBC Television drama about the life of beloved educator and humanitarian Mary McLeod Bethune, which won the Robert E. Sherwood Television Award. He has received the Hannah Del Vecchio award for achievement in playwrighting and a Guggenheim Fellowship for creative writing in drama. The National Conference of Christians and Jews awarded his work a special citation. In 1968, Branch originated, wrote and co-produced a ninety-minute documentary film for National Educational Television entitled "Still a Brother: Inside the Negro Middle Class." It won the American Film Festival Blue Ribbon award for excellence. Currently Branch is working on new projects for theatre and film from his home in New Rochelle, New York.

THEODORE BROWNE is actor, playwright, teacher, born in Suffolk, Virginia, in 1910, educated in New York City's public and high schools and City College of New York with a M.Ed. from Northeastern. He wrote two plays for the Federal Theatre's Negro Company—*Natural Man* and an African version of *Lysistrata*. He was the first Afro-American to receive the Rockefeller Dramatist's Guild Fellowship in playwrighting. Browne's *Natural Man* also had a successful off-Broadway run in New York under the auspices of The American Negro Theatre. He is the author of *Minstrel* and *A Black Woman Called Moses,* both full-length plays; and a novel *The Band Will Not Play Dixie*, published in 1958 by Exposition Press. He now resides, teaches, and lectures in Roxbury, Massachusetts.

ED BULLINS is Playwright in Residence at The New Lafayette Theatre in Harlem under the direction of Robert MacBeth, and also conducts their playwrights workshop. The New Lafayette has presented Mr. Bullins' *In the Wine Time* and *Goin A Buffalo.* The American Place Theatre has presented two Bullins plays, *The Electronic Nigger* and *The Pig Sty.* Much of his earlier work was presented in San Francisco. Ed has traveled in Africa, attended Black Theatre conferences abroad and at home and has the unique position of working full time in the Black community as a playwright. Bobbs-Merrill has published five of his one-act plays.

STEVE CARTER a native New Yorker, was graduated from the High School of Music and Art as an art major. He has been a dancer, photographer, and a designer, but has always considered himself a writer, having written plays since he was fifteen, "a long time ago." He is a Scorpio, born on the seventh day of the eleventh month at 1:17 A.M. and tipped the scales at 11 pounds and 7 ounces in room 171. He wrote plays, designed sets and costumes, taught body movement and operated sound and lights with Maxwell Glanville's American Community Theatre. Steve has written industrial and short-subject films, and *One Last Look* has been performed at The St. Marks Playhouse, and has been seen on ABC-TV's "Like It Is." He is production co-ordinator and director of the playwright's workshop with The Negro Ensemble Company. During the summer of 1969 he managed a highly successful tour of that workshop in their production of *Black Is . . . We Are.*

ALICE CHILDRESS a Charlestonian, began her career as actress, director, and writer at The American Negro Theatre in Harlem, New York City and worked there for twelve years. She is the author of the following produced plays: *Florence, Gold Thru the Trees, Just a Little Simple* (an adaptation of Langston Hughes's first *Simple Speaks His Mind*), *Trouble in Mind* (which won the "Obie"

Award for the best original off-Broadway play of the 1955–56 season). The same play was produced twice by the B.B.C. in London.
She received a Harvard appointment to The Radcliffe Institute for
1966–68, and the University of Michigan presented her play *Wedding Band* as their Professional Theatre Production of 1966, with
Ruby Dee, Abbey Lincoln, and Jack Harkins. She is also the author
of *Martin Luther King at Montgomery, Alabama*, recently completed
The African Garden, and is now working on a novel. She has compiled this collection in answer to the many requests for audition
and class scene study material based upon Black experience.

OSSIE DAVIS actor, playwright, and director, is the author
of *Purlie Victorious*, for stage and screen, co-author (with Arnold
Perl) of the screenplay *Cotton Comes to Harlem* and has written for
television shows . . . "East Side, West Side," and "The Eleventh
Hour." He has acted in *A Raisin in the Sun*, *Purlie Victorious*, *Anna
Lucasta*, *Jeb*, *The Zulu and The Zayda* and many other shows on
and off-Broadway and for motion pictures and television plays. He
is the father of three children and the husband of actress Ruby Dee.
Ossie has been most active in Black community affairs in the United
States and in the cause of world peace and human rights.

ROGER FURMAN is the founder-director of The New Heritage Repertory Theatre, located in Harlem, New York City, has written and directed works performed on the streets of Harlem and in facilities provided by the community. His company performed in I.S.
201 for several seasons. His play *The Gimmick* was done at Columbia
University's School of The Arts in April 1970. Roger Furman is also
a set designer and did the scenes for the motion picture *The Cool
World*. He worked most recently as assistant director to Ossie Davis
in filming *Cotton Comes to Harlem*. He directed his group in the
presentation of two plays by Alice Childress, *Mojo* and *Wine in the
Wilderness* for performances during the season of 1970–71. Without
the aid of grants, Roger has opened a studio workshop theatre on
125th Street in Harlem. The little theatre seats 110 people. Talk
about bootstraps!

LORRAINE HANSBERRY became, at twenty-nine, the
youngest American, the fifth woman, and the only Black dramatist to
win The New York Drama Critics Circle Award for Best Play of the
Year in 1959. *Raisin* has since been produced and published in some
thirty countries and her film adaptation has received numerous
awards. In 1965, at the age of thirty-four, Lorraine Hansberry died
of cancer, while her second play, *The Sign in Sidney Brustein's Win-*

dow was running on Broadway. The first of four volumes of her post-humous work, *To Be Young, Gifted and Black,* has been published by Prentice-Hall. *Les Blancs,* her last major play, became a Broadway production, starring James Earle Jones.

ABBEY LINCOLN Miss Lincoln is the wife of master musician, composer, and drummer Max Roach; and started her career singing with his personal appearances and recordings, especially in the concert presentations of *The Freedom Suite* featuring the song "Africa." She received international rave notices in her films *Nothing but a Man* with Ivan Dixon and *For the Love of Ivy* with Sidney Poitier. Miss Lincoln has appeared in The University of Michigan's professional production of Alice Childress' *Wedding Band* and The WGBH (Boston) television play by the same author, *Wine in the Wilderness,* creating the role of Tommy-Marie. Abbey Lincoln is writing a book and a full-length play, *A Streak o' Lean.*

JULIAN MAYFIELD Born in 1928 in Greer, South Carolina, he was raised and educated in Washington, D.C., enlisted in the peacetime army, and served in the Pacific area; he later studied at Lincoln University. Mayfield has worked as a dishwasher, hack driver, house painter, radio announcer, and newspaperman, but through it all was determined to be a writer. His articles have been printed in *The Nation, Commentary, Negro Digest, Freedomways* and the New York *Times.* His play *417* was produced off-Broadway in New York City. His novels *The Hit* and *The Long Night* have been acclaimed in the U.S.A., Great Britain, and France. Julian Mayfield has acted on Broadway and in several films, recently playing the lead role of *Tank* in *Up Tight,* as well as adapting *The Informer* to Black experience with Ruby Dee and Jules Dassin. Teacher, lecturer, and writer, he is presently an instructor at Cornell University and is working on a book and a film play.

LOFTEN MITCHELL A native of Harlem, he attended New York City public high schools, also Talladega College and Columbia University Graduate School. He is a playwright, screen writer, essayist, and author of a history on one aspect of American Theatre, *Black Drama,* published by Hawthorn Books. Mitchell is the author of the following published plays: *Tell Pharaoh, Land Beyond the River,* and *No Separation.* He also created *Ballad of the Winter Soldiers* (in collaboration with John Oliver Killens), *Ballad for Bimshire* (musical in collaboration with Irving Burgie), *Star of the Morning* and *The Cellar;* and also wrote the films *Integration, Report One,* and *I'm Sorry,* and many articles. He is now completing a play with a most intriguing title *The Final Solution to the Black Problem in the United States of America or The Fall of the American Empire.*

TED SHINE A native of Baton Rouge, Louisiana, he attended the public schools of Dallas, Texas, moved along to Howard University and the State University of Iowa, and is now working toward a Ph.D. at The University of California. In March 1970 he had an off-Broadway presentation of three one-act plays, *Shoes, Plantation,* and *Contribution. Contribution* had been first done by The Negro Ensemble Company of New York City in 1969. His produced plays are *Epitaph for a Bluebird, Morning, Noon and Night, Sho Is Hot in the Cotton Patch, Miss Weaver, Comeback, After the Fire, Idabel's Fortune,* and *Flora's Kisses.* Mr. Shine has also written an all-Black soap opera dealing with urban problems; it was produced by The Maryland Center for Public Broadcasting in Baltimore, Maryland. He has taught and lectured at southern and northern universities and is the recipient of many honors and awards.

DOUGLAS TURNER WARD Actor-director-writer and Artistic Director of The Negro Ensemble Company, he was born on a plantation in Burnside, Louisiana, and grew up in New Orleans. He made his acting mark in *The Iceman Cometh, Lost in the Stars, A Raisin in the Sun, One Flew Over the Cuckoo's Nest, The Blacks, Blood Knot,* and *Coriolanus.* Ward's first produced plays were *Happy Ending* and *Day of Absence* produced by Robert Hooks at The St. Marks Playhouse. The plays won the Vernon Rice Drama Desk and Obie Awards and had a run that lasted over a year. Under his guidance the Negro Ensemble Company is now in its fourth year of production and has completed a national and a European tour. He has continued to write and act while carrying out the managerial duties connected with N.E.C. Douglas Turner Ward has produced the works of Lonne Elder III (*Ceremonies in Dark Old Men*) and Wole Soyinka (*Kongi's Harvest*) plays by other Black writers and also Peter Weiss's *Song of the Lusitania Bogey.*

THEODORE WARD was born in Thibodeaux, Louisiana, on September 15, 1902. As a young man, in Chicago, he worked as a barbershop porter, bellhop and boat boy. Studied short story and poetry under Dr. Louis Zucker in the Extension Division of the University of Utah, then received the Zona Gale Scholarship to the University of Wisconsin. His first major play, *Big White Fog,* was produced by the Federal Theatre (1938) in Chicago. In 1940 he organized The Negro Playwrights Company in Harlem, in association with Langston Hughes, Paul Robeson and Richard Wright. He also aided in forming The Associated Playwrights, The Midwest People's Theatre, and The South Side Center of the Performing Arts Inc. In 1948 he was awarded a Guggenheim Fellowship for creative writing, to finish *John Brown*, later produced at The Eldridge Theatre in New York City. *Our Lan* was produced at The Henry Street Settlement, then on Broadway in 1947 by Eddie Dowling and Louis Singer. Among his published works are *Throwback, Whole Hog or Nothing, Even the Dead Arise*, and *Shout Hallelujah*.

SELECTED BIBLIOGRAPHY

These plays are available in paperback at your local Black community book shops, through the publishers or from The Drama Book Shop, 150 West 52nd Street, New York, New York 10019.

Seydou Badian, *The Death of Chaka* (Oxford University Press).

James Baldwin, *Blues for Mister Charlie* (Dial Press).

William Wells Brown, *The Escape or A Leap for Freedom* (R. S. Wallcut).

Ed Bullins, *Five Plays by Ed Bullins* (Bobbs-Merrill).

——, *How Do You Do?* (Illumination Press).

Aimé Césaire, *A Season in the Congo* (Evergreen).

Alice Childress, *Wine in the Wilderness* (Dramatists Play Service).

J. P. Clarke, *Ozide* (Three Crown Books).

Ossie Davis, *Purlie Victorious* (Samuel French, Inc.).

Lonne Elder III, *Ceremonies in Dark Old Men* (Samuel French, Inc.)

Charles Gordone, *No Place to Be Somebody* (Bobbs-Merrill).

Lorraine Hansberry, *A Raisin in the Sun* (Samuel French, Inc.).

——, *To Be Young, Gifted, and Black: Lorraine Hansberry in Her Own Words*, adapted by Robert Nemiroff (Prentice-Hall).

Langston Hughes, *Five Plays by Langston Hughes* (A Midland Book).

Errol John, *Moon on a Rainbow Shawl* (Evergreen).

LeRoi Jones, *The Baptism* and *The Toilet* (Evergreen).

Maryat Lee, *Dope!* (Samuel French, Inc.).

Loften Mitchell, *Land Beyond the River* (Pioneer Drama Service).

Wole Soyinka, *Kongi's Harvest* (Oxford University Press).

——, *The Trials of Brother Jero* and *The Strong Breed* (Dramatists Play Service).

Douglas Turner Ward, *Happy Ending* and *Day of Absence* (Dramatists Play Service).

The following anthologies are also available:

New Black Playwrights (including Douglas Turner Ward, William

Wellington Mackey, Adrienne Kennedy, Paul Carter Harrison, Ed Bullins), (Avon).

New Plays from the Black Theatre (including LeRoi Jones, Charles H. Fuller, Jr., Ed Bullins, Ben Caldwell, Salimu, Sonia Sanchez), (Bantam Books).

Plays from Black Africa, edited by Frederic M. Litto (A Mermaid Drama Book).

Short East African Plays in English, edited by David Cook and Miles Lee, (Heinemann Educational Books Ltd).

M